Contemporary Japanese Restaurant Design

Contemporary Japanese Restaurant Design

photos by Nacása & Partners Inc.
text by Motoko Jitsukawa
with Cornucopia K. K.

PERIPLUS

Published by Periplus Editions, with editorial offices at 130 Joo Seng Rd, #06-01, Singapore 368357.

ISBN 0-7946-0160-X

Printed in Singapore

Design: Mind Design

Distributors:
North America, Latin America, and Europe
Tuttle Publishing
364 Innovation Drive,
North Clarendon,
VT 05759-9436, USA
Tel: (802) 773 8930
Fax: (802) 773 6993
Email:
info@tuttlepublishing.com
www.tuttlepublishing.com

Japan
Tuttle Publishing
Yaekari Building 3F,
5-4-12 Osaki,
Shinagawa-ku,
Tokyo 141 0032, Japan
Tel: (03) 5437 0171
Fax: (03) 5437 0755
Email: tuttle-sales@gol.com

Asia Pacific
Berkeley Books Pte. Ltd.
130 Joo Seng Road, #06-01,
Singapore 368357
Tel: (65) 6280 1330
Fax: (65) 6280 6290
Email:
inquiries@periplus.com.sg

Right:
A variety of "tricks" is used to create this traditional tea ceremony room in the basement of a modern building. All electrical equipment, from lighting to air conditioners, is concealed by natural materials. In this photo, light filters through the *washi* (handmade paper).

Contents

Introduction
**Contemporary Restaurant
Design in Japan 8**

Part 1
Contemporary Classics 14

Xex 16
Torafuku 22
Chokyaku Yowa 28
Bou's 34
Hana Noren 40
Kuruma 46
Koomon 52

Part 2
Tradition Redefined 56

The River Oriental 58
Kan 62
Tamasaka 66
Jiyugaoka Grill 72
Zabo 76
Togetsusou Kinryu 82
Chashitsu San-an 88
Hika 94
Negiya Heikichi 100
Scorpione 106
Kushi no Bo 110
Kichiri 116

Part 3
Cultural Cohesion 120

Ken's Dining 122
Murata Mitsui 128
Niu 134
Africa 138
Tile 142
Daidaiya Ginza 148
Lee Nang Ha 154
Futong Mandarin 160
Kamonka 164

Epilogue
I Love Restaurants 170

Designers 174

Introduction
Contemporary Restaurant Design in Japan

There is no large city in the world in which a Japanese restaurant cannot be found. In New York, London, Paris, Beijing, and even in Cairo, Japanese dishes such as *sushi*, *yakitori*, *tempura*, and *shabu-shabu* are available. The popularity of Japanese food is in part due to its reputation as a healthy alternative and also owes something to the atmosphere of refinement for which Japanese dining is well known. Far from being a passing fad, Japanese cookery is now an established item on the menu of famous international cuisine.

In Japan itself, new trends in food and in dining itself are constantly emerging. Despite the recession, many restaurants in Japan enjoy full bookings three or four months in advance due to the popularity of the menu and to the innovative design that marks the restaurants themselves.

Historically, the Japanese have always been quick to introduce new tastes into their daily meals. Uniquely, the typical Japanese diet includes dishes taken from the menu of nations as varied as France, Italy, China and various parts of Africa. The traditions of Japanese cookery are alive and well, but there is a real curiosity about food and willingness to try something new. This outgoing approach to food has had a direct and profound influence on the work of restaurant designers in Japan, who are themselves always looking for a more innovative, exciting approach to designing dining spaces.

Sushi restaurants are traditionally designed so that diners face the chef across a counter. A new style of sushi restaurant has appeared in recent years, however, in which diners are seated on sofas and enjoy wine, rather than the conventional *sake*, with their sushi. Some regard this approach to the sushi restaurant as rather precious, but it has caught on with younger diners who are eager to try new things.

The younger generation of Japanese have been brought up surrounded by elements of Western culture. Though they feel a real attachment to Japanese food, they appreciate innovation in both the dishes on the menu and the design of the restaurants they patronize. Since the 1990s, the Japanese food service industry has depended on members of this generation, with their European sense of dining out as entertainment, refined palates, and good eye for restaurant design.

The new style of restaurants has been created for the most part by designers who are a part of the same generation as the diners among whom these establishments are popular. An adventurous approach to design and the use of traditional Japanese styles and materials in innovative settings and combinations has created a revolutionary new school of restaurant design.

Designers today have produced restaurants that offer thrills, sumptuousness, and surprises, but also provide a sense of nostalgia and a relaxing setting. A willingness to combine high tech and modern materials with traditional ones means that the latest designs offer a new take on the forms of the past.

In the1980s, when many of the designers who are now at their peak were beginning their careers, changes were sweeping through the Japanese food service industry. The years of the bubble economy saw a rapid expansion in the scale of the industry, whilst youngsters who once would not have been able to afford to eat in the best restaurants were setting the trends by seeking out the latest fashionable spot. It was during this period that many of the themes still being explored by Japanese chefs and restaurant designers first emerged.

By the end of the 1990s, the styles that first appeared in the decade before were established as the standard for restaurant cuisine and design. This development marks the first time that restaurants in Japan have really set their own standards, rather than slavishly following trends prevalent in the West, by aiming to please the palate and design sense of the average Japanese diner.

There are three main types of restaurant that are representative of this new generation of dining establishments. The first part of the book illustrates one popular style, which employs new materials in a traditional context. Acrylic resin boards used in fittings or for the ceiling, plastic sheeting for the walls, fiber-optic lighting, rough fabric with stainless steel woven into it used as a wall covering: these are some of the synthetic materials that are being used in what are otherwise conventional dining spaces.

One example of this approach can be seen in a restaurant in central Tokyo. This establishment, based on the traditional teahouse, features acrylic resin used as a material for shelving, the rails in which the *fusuma* sliding doors are set and as a casing for the posts scattered throughout the space. This element of transparency allows light to filter into the space from outside. The effect overall is, however, a traditional one that follows many of the conventional forms of teahouse design. The location of this establishment and the use of innovative materials has made this a popular spot with both tourists visiting from abroad and local office workers.

The combination of new materials and traditional style can lend an element of surprise and excitement to a space. In a high class restaurant on the top floor of one Tokyo high rise, the designer has placed a traditional *tsukubai* (stone basin) within a large pool of water made from clear resin. The *tsukubai* brings to mind the smaller version that appears outside the entrance to many traditional teahouses to give guests an opportunity to wash their hands before passing inside. Lights sets below the water draw attention to the uneven surface of the *tsukubai*, whose shadow is cast on the walls of the pool. The walls facing this pool are made in the *hanchiku* style, with white mortar highlighting the interstices between individual stones. The effect overall is one of contrast between rough traditional materials and smooth modern ones, yet this contrast serves to set off both old and new elements.

Another approach that is found in many of today's restaurants is one in which simple materials such as

Overleaf:
Bou's, a modern restaurant in Shinjuku, Tokyo, is lit with green lights, which are set within partitions made from finely crushed wine bottles.

Above left:
The wall and partition of this restaurant, Kushi no Bou, are plastered with earth using a traditional Japanese technique. Designer Yokoi skilfully uses traditional materials to hide modern fittings, such as the lighting equipment in the ceiling, which is covered with delicately woven bamboo net.

Above right:
In this small Japanese restaurant, Murata Mitsui, the walls of the main dining room are covered with 3,500 wooden *sake* measures to interesting effect.

wood, paper, and packed earth are used in innovative ways to give a contemporary feeling to a dining space while adding warmth and harkening back to an earlier age when these materials were the basic building blocks of Japanese construction.

Sometimes technology makes it possible for traditional materials to be used in an entirely new way. Examples include the use of *washi* as a wall covering, in flooring, lampshades, and other unusual places to give a contemporary feeling to this long used material. *Washi* is sturdier than the kind of paper that is commonly used for writing, but it is vulnerable to heat. This led one designer to use fiber optic lighting, which does not emit heat, for a restaurant in which *washi* was extensively used.

A contemporary feeling is sometimes produced by the innovative remodeling of an old building. In the Gion quarter of Kyoto, a number of designers have faced the challenge of refitting classic style buildings in what is an architectural conservation area. This makes for a tight budget, with much of the money in such remodeling projects going towards replacing out-of-date equipment and fixtures. One designer who remodeled an old inn in Kyoto brought it back to life as a contemporary restaurant despite the low budget, leaving many of the more attractive original features in place. The original handrails still grace the stairs, while the original transom and railing round the terrace also remain in place. Modern touches have been added in the form of such things as wall coverings, furni-

ture, and carpeting. Care has been taken to ensure that the old and new elements harmonize and produce a pleasing effect overall.

It might seem easier from a design viewpoint to demolish an old building and begin afresh with something modern, but some designers have risen to the challenge of bringing their vision to a traditional structure. One example is in the form of a tiny, old house surrounded by huge, modern buildings in the middle of Osaka. This has been remodeled using traditional Japanese materials such as *kawara* (roof tiles) and *sake* measures as design motifs. The age and diminutive size of the restaurant, rather than being a handicap, are a draw for the customers.

Another popular trend in restaurant design combines elements of Japanese design with motifs and items borrowed from abroad. Special attention has been given to Asian elements in many of these designs, creating spaces with a pan-Asian appeal that is a unique hybrid.

One designer covered the walls of a stairwell with *tatami* mats, normally used for covering the floor, hanging antique European lampshades in the same space to provide an eclectic atmosphere. In the dining-bar section of the restaurant, two enormous lamps with shades designed to resemble the thatch that covers a traditional Japanese farmhouse take pride of place on a huge dining table. One wall is covered with prints in the Chinese style, while another wall surface is covered with mirrors to open up the space and add light.

The lotus is the design motif of this fashionable Chinese restaurant, Niu. The walls are illuminated in the pink of lotus flowers and the shape and color of lamp shades represent the buds.

The fundamental inspiration for the design is Western, but various Asian elements add a variety and sense of fun that never fails to impress diners. This space is not then truly Western or Asian in style, but rather a concrete expression of the designer's own vision.

In another inspired design, a faux rice fields takes the place of honor in a Korean restaurant. While the rice field would seem to suggest a decidedly Asian slant, the interior of the restaurant blends features from a variety of cultures, including as it does Western furniture and a large photograph of a female nude taken by a well known New York photographer. This space, which was once home to a tile warehouse, manages to bring these elements together to create an attractive environment whose whole is more than the sum of its parts.

One designer featured here suggests that he is more concerned with expressing his idea of Japan than with following traditional or contemporary conventions and focuses on selecting and combining materials that he finds beautiful and interesting.

The generation of restaurant designers now creating some of the leading work in this field all have in common a desire to express the fundamentals of Japanese architecture and design in new ways that suit today's restaurant-goers. It is very likely that the innovative techniques and solutions to complex challenges now being worked out by many of Japan's best restaurant designers will continue to attract growing attention from around the world.

Part 1
Contemporary Classics

One popular style of contemporary Japanese restaurant design introduces high-tech, modern materials into traditional contexts, evoking a sense of adventure and excitement in what are otherwise conventional Japanese dining environments. Some of these restaurant designs feature fiber-optic lighting, fittings, and ceilings made of acrylic resin boards, and wall coverings of plastic sheeting or rough fabric woven with stainless steel. A willingness to use synthetic materials in traditional settings means that these designs offer a new take on the forms of the past.

XEX
Ryu Kosaka
Atagoyama, Tokyo

Atagoyama Hills is one of the new-generation high-rise buildings springing up in Tokyo. Occupying the entire 1,000 square meter (10,764 sq ft) space of the top floor of this building, XEX comprises two restaurants and a bar. Visitors leaving the lift on the 47th storey walk along a marble-floor corridor to the reception desk, where they are warmly greeted and shown to the bar.

The latter is connected to the two restaurants — one Italian and the other Japanese — and is furnished with comfortable sofas and tables separated by wooden latticework.

The three separate sections of the restaurant, each with its own distinct menu and atmosphere, do not limit guests' seating and dining options. If they are dining in the Italian restaurant, for example, they can also order sushi or *sake* from the Japanese restaurant. Hence, guests select their seating by mood rather than menu, and the role of the bar is not only to serve aperitifs but also to allow guests time to select their preferred dining spot.

To pass from the bar to the Italian restaurant, guests are guided through a long corridor, which is lit from above and below by soft light encased in acrylic panels.

The Japanese restaurant is linked to the bar via a narrow, snaking passage with wood-paneled walls and black stepping stones set on white gravel stones.

The designer, Ryu Kosaka, explains that these passageways were designed for dramatic effect.

Left:
The narrow passageway to the Japanese restaurant from the bar is designed like the entrance to an old temple, with white gravel beneath stepping stones.

Plan:
Completed in 2002, the Atagoyama Hills building is one of the most contemporary developments in Tokyo. Located on the top floor of this complex, XEX gives guests a fine view of Tokyo both in the daytime and at night.

"The bar and restaurants are designed in completely different styles. I hope that guests will experience a feeling of anticipation as they move from one area to another, all the while wondering what they will come upon when they arrive."

The entrance area of the Japanese restaurant features a stone wall built in the *hanchiku* style, which makes use of white gravel and cement to create a delicate, irregular texture. Opposite this wall are a number of doors, made of carved *naguri* (traditionally hand carved) wooden boards, leading on to rooms for private parties of between six and ten people. Also near the entrance, a pool of water contained in a clear acrylic pool is set off by a large, rough stone basin, or *tsukubai*, from which water flows into the pool. This *tsukubai*, which allows those taking part in tea ceremonies to wash their hands before entering, was chosen by the designer as a means of providing a contrast with the smooth, straight lines of the acrylic lining of the pool.

The restaurant includes a sushi bar and a counter serving *aburiyaki* (Japanese barbecue) grilled meats and vegetables. Tucked discreetly behind the sushi bar is a VIP room with walls and floor covered with *kakishibu*-coated *washi* (handmade paper dyed with persimmon extract). The partition screens in the room are made of charcoal, which is both an attractive feature and effective at absorbing odor.

Of course, one of XEX's most eye-catching features is the stunning view of Tokyo available from almost every table in the restaurant.

Left top:
The Japanese restaurant is divided into two sections: an *aburiyaki* section and a sushi section. In the former, pictured here, guests watch barbecued dishes being prepared in front of them. The counters are separated by wooden latticework made of wood and charcoal.

Left bottom:
A bonus for guests sitting at the sushi counter is a fine view from the wide window. The simple design of the pale wooden counter does not interfere with the scenery or the food.

Right:
The walls leading to the entrance of the Japanese restaurant have been created using the traditional *hanchiku* process. The irregular surface provides an interesting effect when illuminated from the floor. In the pool, which is made of transparent acrylic boards, the water flows continuously from the *tsukubai*. The sound of water contributes to the sense of calm in the entrance hall.

Guests remove their shoes in the *koagari* section of the restaurant. The small wooden tables are separated by pressed metallic screens, which resemble bamboo netting. Their cool semi-transparent appearance provides guests with a feeling of spaciousness while preserving privacy.

Torafuku
Ryu Kosaka
Toranomon, Tokyo

Located in the atrium of an office building, this casual Japanese-style tavern has a 400 square meter (4,306 sq ft) floor area. Dominating the kitchen are two traditional clay *kamado* (stoves) for cooking rice.

Designer Ryu Kosaka has used traditional Japanese materials in unconventional ways. His emphasis is on simplicity and maintaining the natural appeal of the materials, which he believes gives the overall design a sophisticated feeling.

"The more processed or decorated a space is, the less attractive traditional materials become. It is necessary to expose the natural texture of the materials wherever possible," he says.

The restaurant offers two distinct seating styles; a raised-floor area (*koagari*) where cushions and low tables adorn raised *tatami* (woven straw) mats, and a section of taller tables and high backed chairs (*doma*). The walls of the *koagari* section are plastered with an ochre mud mixed with straw. This popular wall-surfacing technique not only has a pleasing appearance but the materials also deodorize the room. The rustic texture of the walls contrasts with the sleeker, checkered, wooden ceiling.

The flooring here consists of *naguri* (traditionally hand carved) wooden boards, woven bamboo mats, and *washi* (handmade paper), providing guests with various sensations as they walk over the mats in their stockinged feet.

The predominance of natural materials would have resulted in dull uniformity, so Kosaka introduces modern materials such as glass. In a striking example, Kosaka emphasizes the concrete posts in the *tatami* area with glass casings, instead of hiding them behind wood or mud. "This provides a kind of tension within the space," he says.

The design of Torafuku demonstrates the dynamic balance that is achievable through the thoughtful use of both traditional and modern materials.

Above left:
In this room for private parties, guests can feel three different textures with their feet: the irregularly hand cut *naguri* boards, the cool and smooth touch of bamboo nets, and the soft touch of *washi*. The ceiling is covered with a basketwork of thinly sliced wood known as *ajiro*, a traditional style in old aristocratic houses. All these materials are traditional but Kosaka has provided an original twist by introducing new technology to produce them and by using unexpected colors and surfaces.

Above right:
An uneven floor made from small pebbles covers the more casual *doma* section of the restaurant, where wooden tables arranged in rows.

Plan:
The atmosphere of the *koagari* section is like a chic traditional Japanese restaurant, while the *doma* section, where large tables and chairs are situated, is more like a casual tavern.

KITCHEN

MANAGER'S ROOM

PRIVATE ROOM

CLOAK ROOM

RECEPTION

RAISED AREA

OPEN KITCHEN

KAMADO (STOVES)

ENTRANCE

TERRACE

COUNTER

TERRACE

DRINKS PREPARATION AREA

The reception counter comprises a series of wooden boards pressed together and then hand carved with a special chisel, giving a sense of formality to the restaurant.

Cement pillars, normally hidden, are deliberately made conspicuous by glass coverings. The *washi*-covered walls, *tatami*-matted floor, and *ajiro* ceiling are all balanced with the pillars to give this private room a very contemporary feeling.

Chokyaku Yowa
Masaaki Ohashi
Chofu, Tokyo

The name of this restaurant is taken from the title of a story about a fisherman boasting about the size of his catch; the menu accordingly emphasizes salt-water fish. Guests at Chokyaku Yowa cook their own fish over a charcoal fire using *gotoku* (traditional Japanese grills), in a manner that has been popular in Japan for almost 400 years. The owner loves fishing and keeps a boat for the purpose at a small island, about two hours off the Tokyo coast. Even when he is not fishing in the area, the owner has arranged for the local fishermen to send selected items from their catch to the restaurant every day.

From the outside, the restaurant appears like a white boat floating on a blue sea; within, the dining space resembles the interior of a fishing boat. Guests entering the restaurant are greeted both by the savory aroma of grilled fish and the sight of a large brazier under a striking ventilation hood. A number of porthole-like windows dot the walls, which are covered in *washi* (handmade paper) in shades ranging from orange to deep red. These paper surfaces are lit from the back, which produces a sunset-at-sea effect.

The first floor features a large *irori* (sunken hearth), and guests gather around this to place their skewered fish over the hot coals. The wall behind the hearth is also covered with *washi*. A number of smaller *irori* are also located on this floor, with large doughnut-shaped blue partitions, which are deliberately reminiscent of life preservers, providing a degree of privacy.

The atmosphere is friendly and relaxed, and guests sometimes even exchange samples of grilled fish with diners at a neighboring hearth by passing the item through the center of the doughnut-shaped partitions! It is the sophisticated yet simple design of this restaurant that encourages this kind of friendly exchange and sets the tone for Chokyaku Yowa.

Right:
A well placed mirror under the stairs reflects the illumination from the rest of the room, creating a special space.

Below:
"Today's Special" fish are displayed and roasted behind the first floor counter. The large, modern ventilator and ceiling hood creates a dramatic effect.

Opposite:
This semi-circular lamp-shade is made of corrugated cardboard and painted with red ink and *sumi* (Chinese black ink). It hangs from the ceiling, looking like the bottom of a ship. The earth textured wall behind gives a rustic feeling to the space.

Left:
On the second floor, guests
sit around a large *irori*,
and roast fish and shellfish
themselves. Large, blue
donut-shape partitions separate each table.

Plan:
The casual mood of the
tavern attracts a lot of local
guests who regularly visit
and enjoy the relaxed
atmosphere. The design
emphasizes the freshness
and variety of the fish.

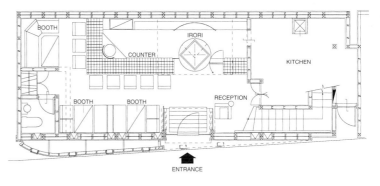

1 F

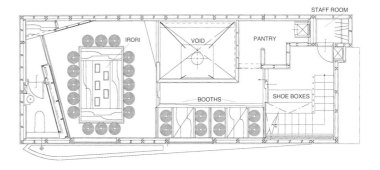

2 F

Bou's
Masaaki Ohashi
Shinjuku, Tokyo

Opposite:
The dim lighting filtering out from corrugated cardboard lampshades lends an intimate atmosphere to this private dining room and stairway to a loft space. *Kakishibu* coated *washi* covers the wall, adding a delicate effect. Ohashi uses both traditional and modern materials here in unconventional ways.

Left below:
The pyramid shape lampshade covered with corrugated cardboard is one of the symbols of the restaurant. Thin, sharp rays of light leak through the joints of cardboard to shine on the floor.

The owner of this restaurant is particularly fond of wine and imports specially labeled wine from his favorite winery in France to serve his guests. He requested that designer Masaaki Ohashi create a place in which people enjoy wine as well as food from a menu featuring an original mixture of French, Italian, and Asian cooking.

The main feature of the restaurant is the emerald green partitions, which are made with finely ground wine bottles suspended in a polyester adhesive. These screens are lit from within, providing a soft green illumination that lends the restaurant an air of fantasy.

A large inverted pyramid-shaped light source points downward from the ceiling at the center of the restaurant, its light filtering through the corrugated cardboard lampshade. This same cardboard appears under the glass surface of each dining table and counter as part of a consistent decorative theme. The tables are woven lengths of split bamboo; spotlights above every table lights each individual dining space. The bamboo is repeated in the flooring for its warmth and tactile appeal.

Delicate screens, of partially translucent fabric that is sandwiched between two pieces of glass, are positioned between the tables to provide some measure of privacy for the diners. "The diffused lighting and the screens produce a relaxed atmosphere in which diners can concentrate on the food, the wine, and the conversation without being distracted," explains Ohashi.

The main dining room is visible from the private dining space of the mezzanine.

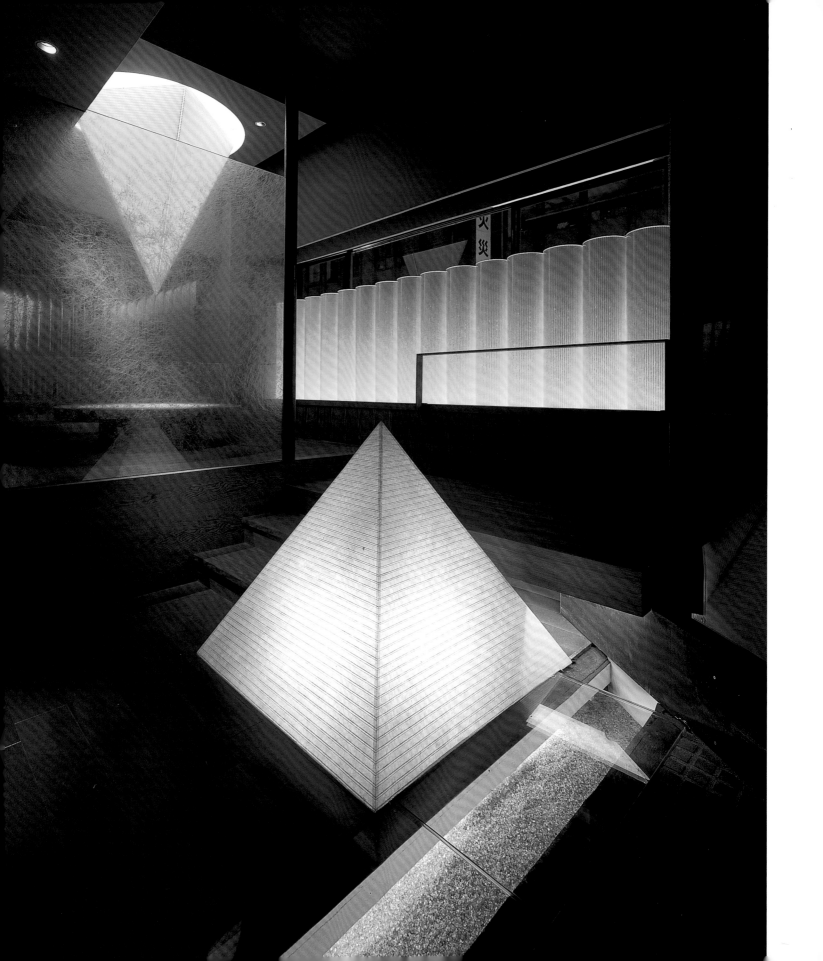

Opposite:
Corrugated cardboard pyramids light the entrance to Bou's.

Right:
This restaurant is lit with green lights, which are set within partitions made from wine bottles that have been ground into small pieces.

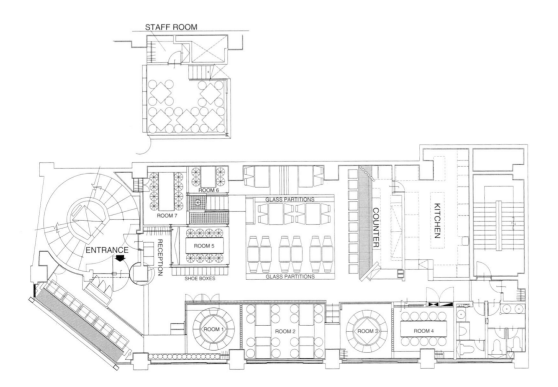

STAFF ROOM

ROOM 6

ROOM 7

GLASS PARTITIONS

COUNTER

KITCHEN

ENTRANCE

RECEPTION

ROOM 5

SHOE BOXES

GLASS PARTITIONS

ROOM 1

ROOM 2

ROOM 3

ROOM 4

Plan:
Although located within the bustling streets of Shinjuku, the atmosphere of the restaurant is calm due to the simple but sophisticated design.

Hana Noren
Masaaki Ohashi
Akasaka, Tokyo

This chic *izakaya* (Japanese tapas bar) is located in Akasaka, one of Tokyo's busiest and most fashionable areas. Many business people stop by at this restaurant after work. The limited floor space of the restaurant did not discourage designer Masaaki Ohashi from breaking up the interior, giving each space a distinct feel. The area near the entrance has a casual mood, evoked by bright lighting encased in corrugated cardboard lampshades, and by bold, simple forms. The predominant materials of wood and concrete used in this space are all in neutral tones.

Past the main dining area, one finds a dimmer and more sophisticated dining section, dominated by *washi*-decorated surfaces.

Another space, about 15 square meters (161 sq ft) in area, is decorated *a la* a Noh stage. The wall is painted black and highlighted by stainless steel rods, about three millimeters (0.1 in) in diameter, applied in a random pattern. Illuminated by footlights, the wall resembles a monochromatic *sumi-e* painting. This is a traditional Chinese painting made using black ink, and the picture suggests rain falling amid a thick mist.

At the deepest point of Hana Noren is a secluded area furnished in one section by large, black tables and chairs and in another by *tatami* (woven straw) mats and low tables. The built-in lighting in the ceiling in this area is shaded with *kakishibu*-coated *washi* (handmade paper dyed with persimmon extract). This results in a subtle illumination that creates an intimate, twilight-like atmosphere.

Dim lighting is provided by *washi* (handmade paper) lampshades on the floor and by *washi*-covered illumination in the ceiling. *Washi*-covered walls make this secluded part of the restaurant chic and elegant. A small space, resembling a Noh stage, adds a dramtic accent to the whole space.

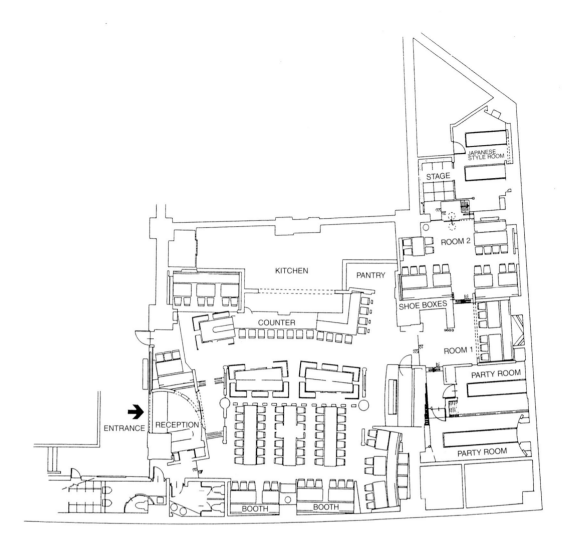

Plan:
The restaurant space is divided into two sections, and the designer uses contrasting materials and illumination to distinguish the mood.

Opposite:
The concrete partition at the entrance is hollowed out in the shape of a moon and filled in with bamboo lattice-work, which is traditionally used in Japanese gardens. The large corrugated cardboard lampshade suspended from the ceiling softens the modern style of the floor.

Right:
The bright lighting and casual atmosphere of the restaurant entrance attract business people after office hours.

Far right:
The floor is laid with boards of three colors. The mosaic pattern of flooring sets a casual mood for the main dining space

To the rear of the restaurant, Ohashi has created a small stage similar to that in a Noh drama, and named it Tenku no ma, or "Sky Room." The walls are covered with unwoven black fabric and thin stainless steel rods, which, when illuminated from the bottom, produce the effect of raindrops falling from the sky .

Kuruma
Gen Yokoi
Shinjuku, Tokyo

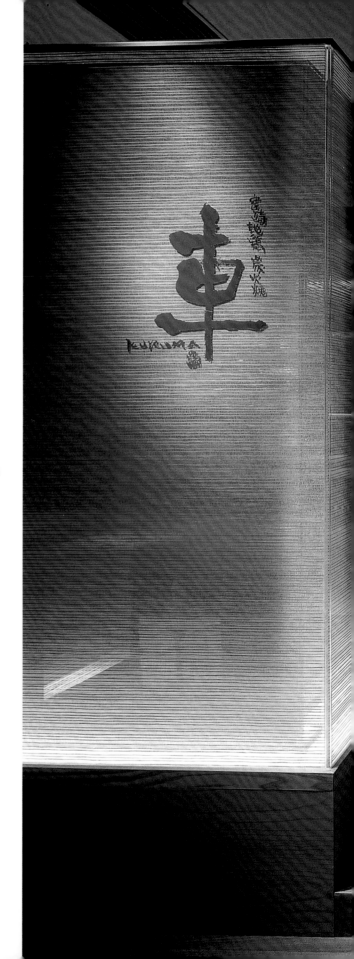

Located in a modern commercial building in Shinjuku, this elegant *yakitori* (grilled chicken) restaurant combines traditional natural materials with original modern ones. The space is not extensive — in fact, the ceiling is low and the floor area is limited — but designer Gen Yokoi has adopted some unique ideas to give it a spacious and relaxed feel, and an exquisite and stylish design.

To disguise the fact that the diners are in close proximity to the building's elevators, Yokoi surrounded the entrance with a unique material: a fabric spun of silver thread. This material is sandwiched between two sheets of glass, resulting in glittering panels that veil the interior and separate the tranquil dining space from the busy exterior, and that enliven the whole space. These screens are balanced by plain wood — the other key material used in the restaurant design.

The rustic old wood beams stretching across the ceiling contrast with the delicate design of tables and chairs. Guests sitting on the specially designed low chairs and stretching their legs into the lowered floor under the table are not aware of the low ceiling. They appreciate instead an abstract image of sunset painted on cloth and attached to the ceiling of the *tatami*-matted room.

"A restaurant is a space where guests can forget daily life and enjoy dining in a casual and relaxing setting. Combining traditional and contemporary materials with unexpected ideas makes it possible to create such a space," said Yokoi.

The approach between the elevator hall and the restaurant is flanked by double layered glass partitions incorporating silver threaded fabric. These translucent screens not only look chic but also provide privacy for the guests inside.

Opposite:
Through the partition, the main dining room can be seen with its tables of plain wood.

Right:
The rustic touch of old wooden beams across the ceiling contrasts beautifully with the rest of the elegantly designed space.

Plan:
Yokoi's design maximizes the use of space without making customers feel cramped. The seats are hollow, allowing guests to store their belongings, and translucent partitions separate the diners without boxing them in.

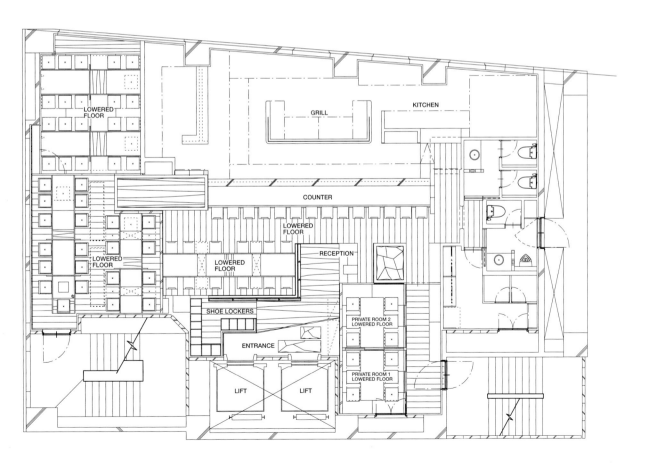

An abstract image of sunset painted on cloth is pasted on the low ceiling of the restaurant. The floor is lowered under the table and guests can sit on the low chairs without having to cross their legs.

Koomon
Fujio Takayama
Nihonbashi, Tokyo

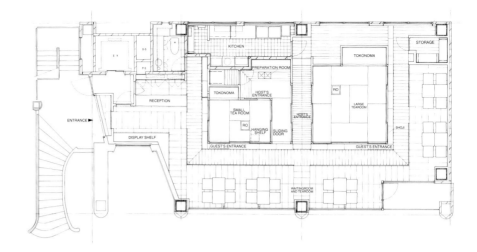

In this restaurant, the designer, Fujio Takayama, has chosen to use modern materials within the context of a traditional teahouse. Located within an office building in central Tokyo, this teahouse was built by a company specializing in tea utensils with a view to popularizing the Japanese tea ceremony. Its convenient location makes it possible for foreign visitors to experience the tea ceremony and for local office workers to enjoy drinking tea in the traditional manner.

Takayama was given the mandate to use new materials and styles to enunciate some of the traditional elements of teahouse design. This approach has resulted in some striking features, such as the use of transparent acrylic throughout the restaurant — in the posts, in the rails on the sliding doors, in the ceiling and for the shelves.

This novel design produces an airy effect, and the sliding doors and shelves appear to float in midair without any support. Thin, rectangular pieces of *washi* (handmade paper) are layered upon one another and applied to the ceiling. The contours of the paper are sharply defined by the light shining through from behind.

Traditionally, no forms of artificial lighting are allowed for the tea ceremony, with only the sun or the moon being considered appropriate sources of illumination. To produce the effect of dim, natural light seeping into a traditional teahouse, Takayama uses *fusuma* (sliding doors made of paper). The acrylic material in the doors allows light to filter in from outside. Combined with the fiber-optic lighting that spotlights the large tea bowls used in the tea ceremony, this arrangement provides a dramatic lighting arrangement.

For those unaccustomed to sitting with knees folded for an extended period of time, Koomon is an opportunity to enjoy the ceremony from the relative comfort of chairs, situated outside the *tatami*-matted rooms. With the *fusuma* removed, guests can have an unhindered view of the proceedings.

Plan:
The space consists of two main tea ceremony rooms, a casual tearoom, and a kitchen and shop. Guests can participate in a formal tea ceremony or just have casual tea and sweets.

Left:
The ceiling is covered with *washi* and acrylic board through which soft light permeates. The *washi* is used to conceal the artificial lighting.

Opposite:
The main tea ceremony room is separated from the corridors and the casual tearoom by *fusuma*. Light shines through the transparent acrylic pillars and ceiling. Apart from the liberal use of acrylic, designer Takayama has stuck to very traditional material in the rest of the space.

Above:
When a formal tea ceremony is being held, the sliding partitions are pulled across to block the light from the corridor and the street beyond. These partitions are covered with *washi* in a gradated greenish color made from natural dyes.

Right:
Tradition and modernity fuse in the simple tea ceremony rooms. The designer solves the problem of how to express a natural feeling in the midst of a contemporary building by using a mixture of modern and very traditional materials.

Part 2
Tradition Redefined

A second innovative approach to restaurant design uses traditional materials such as wood, paper, and packed earth in original ways, lending a contemporary air to dining spaces while looking to an earlier age when natural materials were the essential elements of Japanese construction. Technological progress has made it possible for *washi* (handmade paper) to take on new uses as a floor or wall covering, giving traditional materials a modern feel. Some of these designs involve refitting classic buildings, so as to ensure that the old and new elements harmonize and produce a pleasing overall effect.

The River Oriental
Ichiro Sato
Kiyamachi, Kyoto

Overleaf:
Although the lounge in
Hika is furnished in a simple
western style, both the
washi-covered wall and the
shoji are reminiscent of a
traditional Japanese house.

Opposite:
Sato has kept the basic
fittings of this more than
60-year-old building, making
use of the exquisite latticework above the wooden
terrace and the extra wide
window panes, but repaint-
ing the walls in matte white.

Below:
The former inn, Funatsuru,
is reborn as a fashionable
restaurant and banquet
hall, after having undergone
only minimal renovation.

The building housing The River Oriental restaurant
was once home to the Funatsuru Inn, which featured
one of the most popular and fashionable banqueting
halls in Kyoto in its day. Constructed in 1930, the
structure was originally scheduled to be razed to
make way for a taller block, but zoning regulations
prevented a high-rise building from being constructed.

The decision was thus made to re-model the
space as a restaurant and a wedding banquet room.
The designer, Ichiro Sato, had to keep costs associated with interior design down, as most of the
budget was being used for reinforcement and renovation works.

This presented the designer with the challenge
of making the best use of the building's original
features while adding touches that give the whole
a suitably fashionable appearance. Some of the
original fittings left in place include the *ramma* (decorative transom), the attractively carved handrails
of the staircase, and the railing round the terrace.
The floors are now covered with a carpet of a unique
design, while the walls are recovered with blackened iron sheeting.

Sato took pains to ensure that the new furniture
and modern fittings did not make the existing features look shabby. "When mixing original features
and new materials, it is important to select materials
that complement the original. I chose new elements
that I thought somehow embodied the feeling of
a stylish hotel of the 1930s," he said. The result is
a modern edifice with a striking heritage.

Opposite:
The restaurant is furnished with tables and chairs made in a Southeast Asian style; the dishes are Californian, and the fittings are classic Japanese. Hence, guests have a feeling of statelessness.

Above left:
The lower half of the walls is covered with iron sheeting, blackened through heating to a high temperature with a blowtorch. It gives an old fashioned accent to the newly painted white walls. The carpet, couch, and tables are all original designs by Sato.

Above right:
The furniture has been designed to appear old and well-used. This balances with the more traditional features, such as the original banister rails and lighting.

Plan:
From the spacious entrance, guests are lead to a lounge which adjoins a terrace facing the river. While the overall layout is spacious and open, the dining room is clearly segregated.

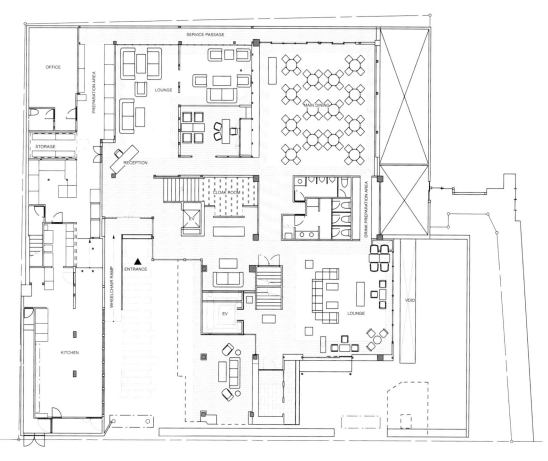

Kan
Ichiro Sato
Ikejiri Ohhashi, Tokyo

There is an air of luxury and relaxation about Kan, despite the fact that the seating area is only 80 square meters (861 sq ft) and has space for just 24 diners. Designer Ichiro Sato was asked to ensure that the layout of the restaurant was similar to that at a tea ceremony, in that the chefs presented dishes directly to diners, and in a formal manner.

This request is realized in a simple and modern design, featuring a counter lined with seats. Chefs prepare dishes at the bidding of the guest, who can watch the cooking process in a way similar to that in a sushi bar.

Sato explains that his goal was to "make the design simple yet sophisticated." To achieve this, he keeps the materials used to a minimum. Cherry wood is used for the counter and chairs; copper covers the ceiling; and packed earth is used for the walls and floor. An attempt has also been made to ensure that everything appears authentic and well used; the pieces of furniture are chosen more for their character than their perfection. The small space is also given a sophisticated feel by the use of simple patterns where materials are shown in their raw state wherever possible.

The most brilliant decoration in this elegant restaurant, however, must be the "natural" view from a big glass window at the entrance. Through this window, guests can appreciate a row of cherry trees growing along the river, which flows in front of the restaurant, as they sample their food, imbibe their drinks, and engage in conversation.

Opposite:
Sato uses three main materials in this small restaurant: copper sheeting in the ceiling; cherry wood in the counter and chairs; and earth in the walls and floor.

Right:
The style of the restaurant is simple. Chefs prepare dishes behind an open counter, allowing guests to view the process and talk with them at the same time. The delicate scent of the cherry wood counter whets the diners' appetite.

Plan:
The restaurant comprises two counters: a long one for dining and another square shaped counter for drinking. Established in 1998, the restaurant has always been packed with business people after work.

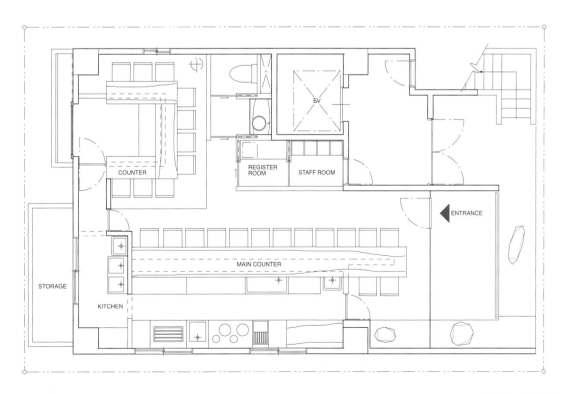

COUNTER

EV

REGISTER ROOM

STAFF ROOM

ENTRANCE

MAIN COUNTER

STORAGE

KITCHEN

Tamasaka
Ichiro Sato
Nishi Azabu, Tokyo

Nishi Azabu is one of Tokyo's more fashionable areas and home to a considerable number of small, sophisticated restaurants. Despite being quite near Roppongi, an area bustling with nightclubs and bars, Nishi Azabu retains a quiet, residential feeling.

Tamasaka is, like many other restaurants in the area, located in what was formerly a private home; hence it is difficult to identify it as a restaurant from the street. The three-storey structure is outwardly minimalist, with a simple garden featuring a cherry tree and Japanese maple that offset the entrance. "Guests get a sense of the changes of the seasons from the garden," says designer Ichiro Sato.

The restaurant has a simple and modern Japanese-style design; it makes use of a small palette of neutral colors as well as natural materials such as bamboo, wood, and paper. There are six small rooms and one large room that features a counter fronted by 10 seats. From their seats at the counter, guests can look out onto a picturesque entrance garden.

Each of the rooms is designed in a different way. One is in a formal *shoin-zukuri* style, with *tatami* (woven straw) mats on the floor and a *tokonoma* (recessed alcove for a flower arrangement or hanging scroll) can be displayed. Another room has tables and chairs set on wooden floorboards. The highlight of this space is the imported stained glass windows from England. This type of windows was popular in the Taisho era of the early 1920s, when a number of impressive Western-style houses, known as

yokan, were built in Japan. The Taisho style was representative of the fusion of Japanese design and Western motifs, which was gaining popularity at the time.

The Taisho theme is expressed by Sato through the use of carefully selected materials and colors, rather than through overt decorative elements, which would serve to distract diners from the food and their conversation.

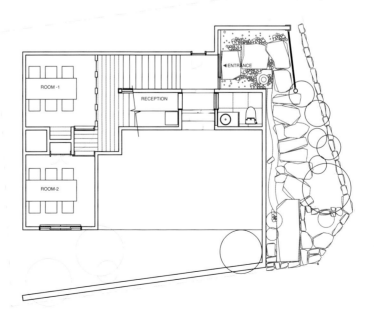

When seated at the long
counter on the first floor,
guests can view a small
garden of maple trees just
outside. Surrounded by a
low wooden ceiling and
earth walls, the atmosphere
is very relaxed.

Plan:
The first floor consists of a
single counter with 10 seats.

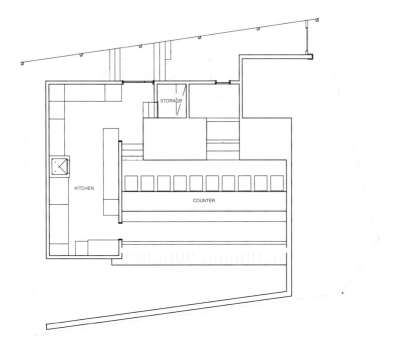

KITCHEN

STORAGE

COUNTER

Opposite:
The design and the use of materials in the six private dining rooms vary from room to room, but all are very simple in style. For example, in this Bamboo Room, the ceiling and the walls are all covered with split bamboo, with just a table and lowered floor. No chairs are needed.

Plan:
Four different styles of private dining room, with space for four to eight people, make up the second floor. Guests choose their room by size and atmosphere.

Above left:
The style of lighting and the stairway are similar to that in a contemporary Japanese residence, although the quality of cooking and service is that of a traditional Japanese restaurant.

Above right:
In the Taisho era (1912–1925) room, western style is combined with traditional Japanese. Stained glass imported from England suggests a tasteful touch of the "good old days" in Japan.

Jiyugaoka Grill
Ichiro Sato
Jiyugaoka, Tokyo

The designer of this space, Ichiro Sato, has planned for a casual dining environment that would encourage couples or groups to drop by after work or on their days off to enjoy homestyle Japanese cooking.

Located in a two-storey modern house in an upmarket residential area in Tokyo, the restaurant looks much like the other homes in the neighborhood from the outside. In fact, passers-by might not realize that the Jiyugaoka Grill is a restaurant, were it not for the huge windows that allow a view of the kitchen from the street.

The interior of the restaurant is free of partitions, which gives it an airy and spacious feel. From anywhere on the ground floor, guests can see the entire restaurant and even gain a partial view of the floors above. "I wanted to recreate the feeling of a family home in which Japanese and European elements are mixed, to provide a relaxed feel overall," says the designer.

Beneath the staircase that leads from the ground floor to the second level is a sitting area where guests can congregate. On the first floor, *shoji* (Japanese sliding doors) consisting of only the wooden frames are placed between the tables. The off-white walls of the restaurant act as an effective backdrop for the mahogany-colored wooden fittings and floor surface.

In the day, the large windows ensure sufficient lighting for the interior, while during the evening hours, the lights within cast a warm glow onto the street, as if encouraging people to enter.

Above:
A house-restaurant with a glassed-in kitchen extension warmly welcomes guests in this Tokyo residential area.

Left:
The interior of the restaurant as viewed from the back door. The white color of the stone contrasts beautifully with the mahogany brown of the wood.

Opposite:
The ground and first floors are connected by a white stairway, but guests can view almost the entire space once they step inside the restaurant, as the area is free of walls. Guest can relax in a space with furniture familiar to that in their own home.

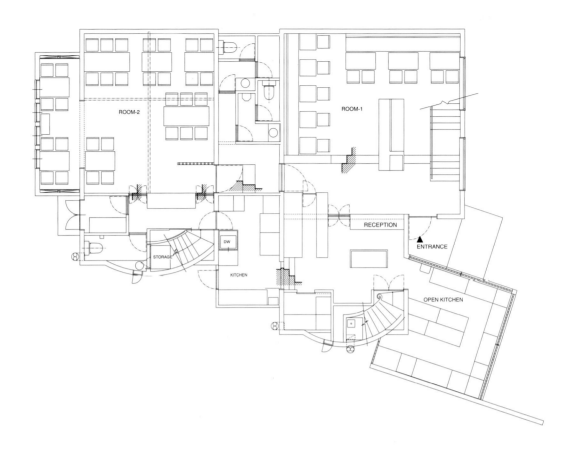

Plan:
The design of the restaurant is that of an ordinary contemporary house in Japan: guests relax in the casual dining space and enjoy brunch, as if in their own living room.

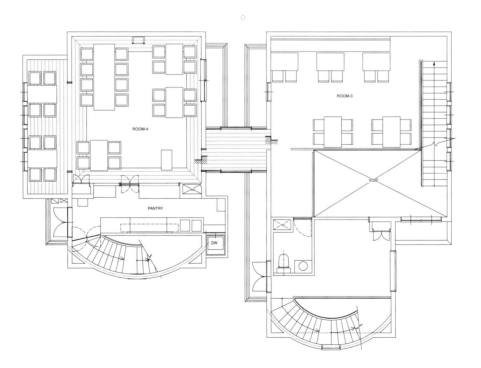

Right:
From the reception, both the first and second floor dining rooms are visible.

Far right:
The contrasting colors of the floor, tables, and chairs (mahogany brown) and the walls (matte white) represent modern Japanese taste, though the design of the furniture is very western. The homelike atmosphere is expressed by the soft illumination from pendant and desk lamps.

Left:
The partitions for each table are similar to frames of *shoji*, which give diners a sense of being comfortably separated from other groups, and without feeling claustrophobic.

Zabo
Ichiro Sato
Shizuoka City, Shizuoka

This restaurant is located in a modern three-storey
building in central Shizuoka, which is 100 kilometers
(62 miles) west of Tokyo. Shizuoka is famous for
its fabulous views of Mount Fuji along its beautiful
beaches and hot-spring resorts, which have attracted
visitors for hundreds of years.

As befits its location, Zabo is designed in the
style of a Southeast Asian resort, in what seems in
part an effort to take advantage of the city's reputation as a tourist destination.

Each floor of the restaurant is designed in a different style, with the ground floor featuring a stylish
bar with a counter and banquettes. The first floor is
divided into small Japanese-style rooms with *tatami*
(woven straw) mats. On the second floor are several
rooms overlooking a garden decorated with stones
and a small pond, reminiscent of an Asian resort. All
rooms have a commanding view of the city.

The garden is symbolically important, according
to the designer. "Even though the building is in an
urban area, guests can forget the hustle and bustle of
city life and relax in the atmosphere of an exotic
resort," says Sato.

Various materials, such as *teppei* stone, are used
throughout the design to add a sense of unity. The
green-blue color of the stone, in combination with
the brown of the wooden fixtures, adds a rustic feel.
The sound of the waterfall that cascades from the
second floor down to the ground level takes guests'
minds away from their hectic lifestyles and invites
them to lose themselves into the relaxed space.

Opposite:
While each floor has different style, their designs are united by certain common elements. One is *teppei* stone, which is used as a decorative material in Japanese houses and gardens. Its lustrous greenish black color gives a rich appearance to the floor and the stairways.

Right:
The Asian resort mood is emphasized by a waterfall running from the second to the ground floor.

Far right:
Southeast Asian lampshades, in a variety of shapes, are dotted around the building.

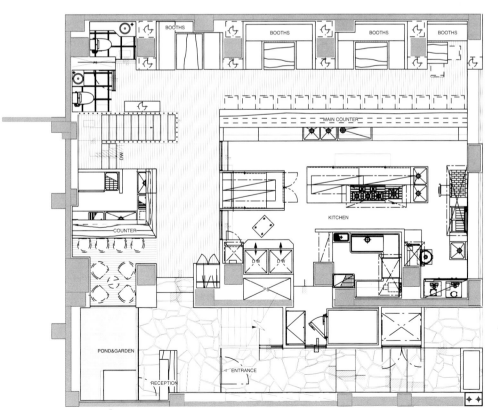

Plans (this page and next):
In this resort-style restaurant, guests can enjoy three different "flavors." They can visit the ground floor for drinks and chic *hors d'oeuvres* at the bar, then proceed to sample delicious Japanese *otsumami* (snacks) served on the first floor, or a Japanese-style dinner on the second floor, which has a view of the garden.

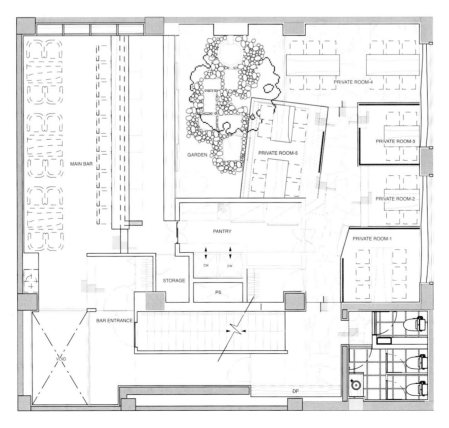

Above:
The bamboo covered wall, the garden of tropical plants, and the choice of ornaments combine to create the atmosphere of an Asian style resort.

Togetsusou Kinryu
Hisanobu Tsuji
Izu, Shizuoka

Oppsite:
The floorboards are made of pinewood and carved by hand using a special chisel and a traditional technique in Japanese architectural design, known as *naguri*. This is a skill few artisans retain today.

Left:
The restaurant looks out onto a beautiful Japanese garden of the original inn constructed 150 years ago.

Togetsusou Kinyru is located within an inn that was built about 150 years ago. There was, at one point, plans to tear down the building and put up a modern edifice in its place, but interior designer Hisanobu Tsujimura argued that it would be easier to attract guests to a traditional inn than to a modern hotel like any other, and also pointed out that craftsmanship of the kind found in the original building could no longer be reproduced.

"I emphasized simple materials and limited the variety of materials used in order to produce a relaxing atmosphere," the designer explains. Two of the main materials used are pine, which is found in the floorboards and tables, and *washi* (handmade paper), which covers the ceilings and walls. The floorboards are carved by hand, which gives them a slight unevenness. The *washi*, which has been dyed an understated beige, adds to the rural, handcrafted feel of the space. The restaurant is illuminated in part by light shining through this paper, which throws the thick fibers making up the cloth-like sheaves into sharp contrast and thereby produces an almost abstract effect.

Tsujimura has worked hard to introduce high technology into the traditional restaurant design, including a flexible, fiber-optic lighting system. This system, in which the lights do not emit any heat, allows staff to control the lighting throughout the restaurant from a central location. The overall effect at Kinryu is one of refined traditional design underpinned by sophisticated technology.

Above:
The approach to the entrance is a narrow patio made of limestone. The walls are plastered, balancing with the natural scenery of the garden.

Overleaf:
The restaurant space can be
divided in two by sliding
doors. The walls and ceiling
are covered with especially
wide *washi*, through which
soft light shines.

Opposite:
Washi colored with natural
dyes cover the walls. When
lit from behind, the uneven
surface of the paper has
a surreal effect on the room.

Right:
The toilet and utility space
are hidden away.

Plan:
The restaurant is in a part of
a large inn, and guests can
dine after taking an *onsen*
(hot spring bath). Designer
Tsuji paid attention to
creating a calm atmosphere
through the use of tradi-
tional natural materials and
contemporary technology.

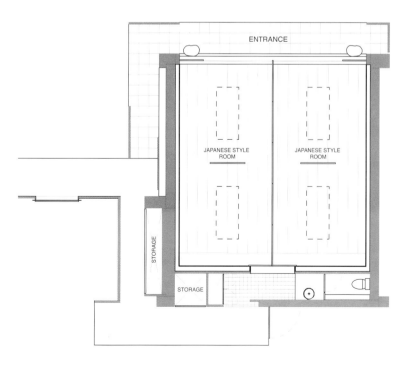

Chashitsu San-an
Fujio Takayama
Kagurazaka, Tokyo

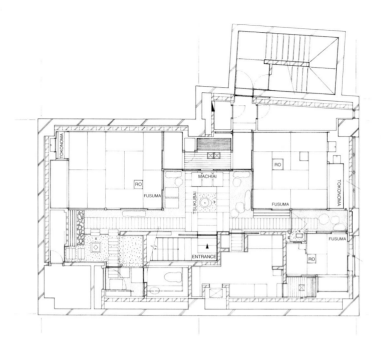

The design of the teahouse, with its rustic features that are meant to encourage humility and contemplation among those taking part in the tea ceremony, has long been one of the strongest influences on Japanese architecture. Formal tea ceremonies have been held in these specially designed spaces since the 16th century.

"Chashitsu San-an," built with the customary tea ceremony in mind, can be roughly translated as a teahouse designed in the style of a mountain hermitage. The owner asked designer Fujio Takayama, an aficionado of the Japanese tea ceremony, to create a formal, quiet space for imbibing tea in the traditional manner — a formidable task given a location in central Tokyo.

Traditionally, the interior of a teahouse features only a *ro* (sunken hearth) and *tatami* (woven straw) mats in a small room where the tea is made and served. Modern features such as light fixtures and air-conditioning are normally eschewed. This tradition presents a challenge for any contemporary designer of spaces to be used for tea ceremony.

In Chashitsu San-an, guests descend a stairway made of *sabi* stone, which contains considerable amounts of iron and will change from a steel grey color to a warmer brown over time. The walls of the stairway are finished with pine boards hand carved in the *naguri* style. The irregular surface of the walls is emphasized by lights shining up from the base, giving guests the illusion that they are moving along a narrow mountain path.

Above:
Positioned centrally in the entrance hall is a *tsukubai* made from *sabi* stone. The chestnut board wall (left in picture) is hand carved using the *naguri* technique. A seasonal flower hangs from the wall.

Plan:
The space consists of three tea ceremony rooms (of ten, eight, and two *tatami* mats) and a kitchen. Due to the convenient location, the space is used not only for formal tea ceremonies but also for casual parties.

The ceiling of the eight-*tatami* mat tea ceremony room is covered with finely knitted bamboo basket weave to conceal the modern lighting. It also provides a contemporary feel to this otherwise traditionally designed room.

A narrow path of stepping-stones leads guests to the eight-*tatami* mat tea ceremony room. Light from the outside leak through the *washi*-covered windows cut in the wooden wall.

Left:
Descending the *sabi* stone stairs, flanked by walls of pinewood board hand-carved with the *naguri* technique, guests feel totally separated from the hustle and bustle of the world outside.

Below:
The ten-*tatami* mat room is designed as a *shoin-zukuri* (traditional Japanese guest-room), with a *tokonoma* (recessed alcove) and shelves. The ceiling is covered with cedar wood board and the light shines through acrylic boards pasted with *washi*.

In the entrance area, or *machiai*, where guests are greeted by their host, a *tsukubai* (stone fountain) provides visitors an opportunity to wash their hands before entering the inner sanctum.

Guests pass from the *machiai* area into one of three rooms either ten, eight, or two *tatami* mats in size. They walk through *fusuma* (sliding doors made of paper) in winter months or a screen woven from reeds in summer.

Takayama has employed a variety of techniques to replicate the atmosphere of a tea ceremony room in the basement of this modern building. All the modern equipment, from lighting to air conditioner, is concealed by natural materials. The light flows through *washi* (handmade paper), and the kitchen is completely hidden from view. An essential element of Japanese tea ceremony is the feeling of "infinite space." Ceilings are high and decorations sparse so as not to disrupt the calm of the ceremony.

Takayama designed Chashitsu with flexibility in mind. The space is not limited in use to formal tea ceremony but easily adapts to a Japanese style dinner party with diners seated on *tatami* mats. The *fusuma* separating the six and eight *tatami* mat rooms can be removed to create a space for over 20 guests.

Delicate screens, with partially translucent fabric sandwiched between two glass pieces, are positioned between the tables for privacy. The diffused lighting and the screens produce an ideal environment for the diners to eat, drink, and converse without feeling distracted.

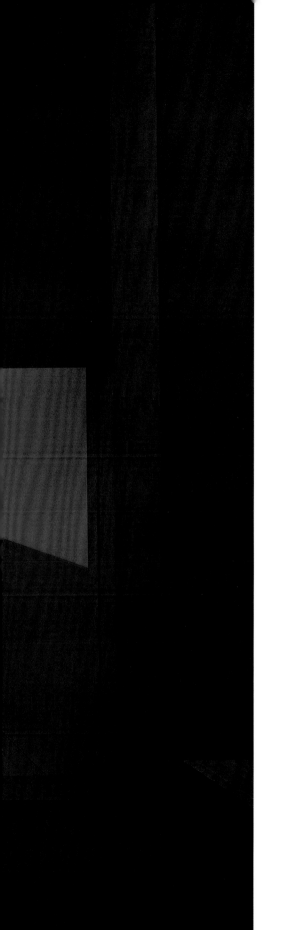

Above:
In front of the narrow entrance to the eight-*tatami* mat room, waiting guests sit on a wooden bench beside a *chozubachi* (hollowed-out stone filled with water for washing hands).

Left:
The two-*tatami* mat room features a naturally carved wood pillar and an *ajiro* ceiling, which is covered with dried cattail grass and cedar wood.

Hika
Yukio Hashimoto
Gion, Kyoto

Located in Gion, which is famous for its elegant restaurants and traditional *machiya* (terraced) *geisha* houses, the building in which Hika is located was built more than 100 years ago.

When refurbishing the interior, designer Yukio Hashimoto had to contend with strict preservation laws, which prohibit substantial structural alterations to traditional buildings in the area. He managed to introduce a radically new interior — a simple, modern space — within the confines of an old building.

"Kyoto is filled with both very old and very new buildings, and I was looking for a way to harmonize tradition and modernity in this house," he says. When guests open the old-fashioned narrow wooden door, they are likely to be surprised by the modern interior of this exclusive club, which features reflective materials, such as glass, marble, and gold foil.

A huge marble *tsukubai* (stone basin) on the ground floor is filled with water, which has cascaded down from a point near the ceiling. Sheets of glass sandwiched with pieces of gold foil add to the sleek feel of the space, as do partitions made of stainless steel and a wall of *washi* (handmade paper) lit from behind. These hard, reflective surfaces heighten the contrast between the wooden exterior of the house and the space within. The space is not extensive, but the diversity of materials and colors used provides a sense of drama and demonstrates the designer's success in fusing the contemporary and the traditional.

Opposite:
From the outside, this house appears to have remained the same for the past 100 years. It is thus difficult to imagine that designer Hashimoto has transformed this traditional teahouse into a contemporary nightclub.

Left:
This *tatami*-matted room is on the first floor of the restaurant. *Washi* covers wall of the *tokonoma* (recessed alcove), and the lowered floor under the table allows guests to sit with legs extended.

Opposite:
In the entrance hall, water flows constantly from the big square shaped *mikage* stone *tsukubai*. The stairs are made of glass and illuminated from within. This illuminated dining space contrasts dramatically with the traditional outward appearance of the house.

Plan:
Hika attracts a fashionable crowd of people. In the lounges in the basement and the ground floor, contemporarily designed furniture sit in rooms with *washi*-covered walls, while the first floor contains *tatami*-matted rooms and a bar.

Right top:
A partition covered with gold foil is used in the basement. The *tsukubai*, located in the illuminated entrance hall, can just be glimpsed beneath the partition.

Right below:
The wall of this *tatami*-matted room on the first floor is covered with *washi* lit from behind with light coming through geometrically cut holes. The large table made from a single piece of cherry wood gives a rustic accent to this chic room.

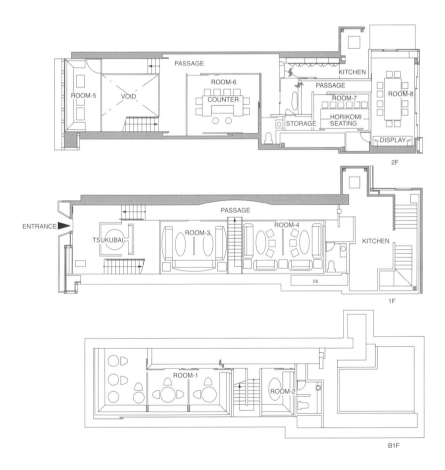

The lounge is viewed through patterned glass that gives the impression of falling raindrops, as if in a *ukiyo-e* (Japanese woodblock) painting.

Negiya Heikichi
Toshiya Kobayashi
Shibuya, Tokyo

Below:
The bar counter on the
ground floor combines modern shelves with back lighting with a well-used wooden
counter and rustic wooden
benches.

Opposite:
Folkloric dolls, dishes and
other artifacts common
in Japanese houses of the
Taisho era (1912-1925) deco-
rate Negiya Heikichi. Guests
enter through the door
to the left of the reception
tansu. The kitchen is to
the right. The contemporary
outward appearance of the
two-storey RC (Reinforced
Concrete) building is in
sharp contrast to the inside
image of an old farmhouse.

Shibuya is one of the liveliest areas of Tokyo, but
Negiya Heikichi, an *izakaya* (Japanese tapas bar)
situated here, is in a relatively quiet area at the edge
of the district. Behind its nondescript, box-shaped,
two-storey concrete facade lies a rich interior, which
could have been found in a wealthy Japanese farmhouse a century ago. It has aged timber beams
and antique chests and other furniture, all of which
provide an atmosphere redolent of the past.

The reception desk consists of an antique *tansu*
(chest). Through a wooden grille to the right of this,
one can see the kitchen. A large bowl of *negi*
(leek) is displayed near the entrance as a symbolic
reminder of the restaurant's name.

In a bar area on the ground floor, staff offer *sake*
and other tipples from behind a long wooden
counter. The old-fashioned, somewhat ponderous
look of the counter and the wooden seats lined up
alongside it in sharp contrast to the back-lit glass
shelves lined with *sake* bottles behind the bar. An
irori (sunken hearth) and the stairway leading to the
first floor are situated beyond the bar.

The patina of the wooden stairs is illuminated
by ceiling lights in antique lampshades. If a guest
glances out of the window near the staircase, he will
see bright neon signs on the buildings opposite, a
marked contrast to the antique feel of the interior.

On the first floor, areas covered in *tatami* (woven
straw) mats can be divided to accommodate groups
of various size with sliding partitions. The windows
are shielded by *shoji* (Japanese sliding doors) of

A reproduction of the traditional Japanese farmhouse
fireplace is positioned opposite the bar counter. *Negi*
is displayed in a traditional
bamboo basket.

washi (handmade paper) on a wooden grill in the traditional fashion, with many of the squares of paper
having been deliberately torn to add a lived-in look.

Designer Toshiya Kobayashi has aimed at
combining modern elements with an old-fashioned
ambience. He placed antiques of the type that would
once have been found in a Japanese farmhouse
within the space for their own value, not with the
intention of turning the restaurant into a repository
of folk design, he says. Also, popular folklore decorations, such as dolls or dishes, which were once
seen in ordinary people's house up until the Taisho
era, some 80 years ago, are dotted around the
space. Tradtional lighting, of a type seen in Japanese
houses 150 years ago, features *washi*-covered lampshades and fills the space with soft, dim light.

The straight lines of the concrete building holding
the warm, farmhouse-style interior that make up
Negiya Hekichi represent a new development in
Japanese restaurant design.

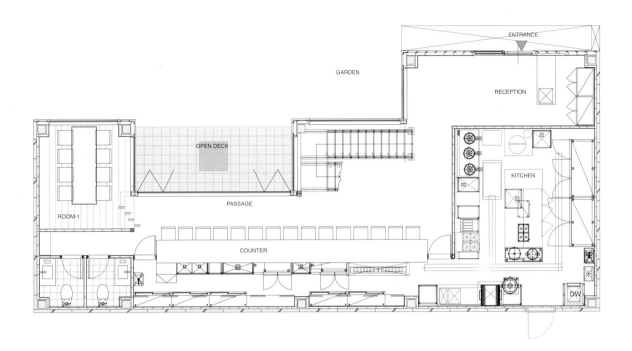

GARDEN

OPEN DECK

PASSAGE

ROOM-1

COUNTER

ENTRANCE

RECEPTION

KITCHEN

DW

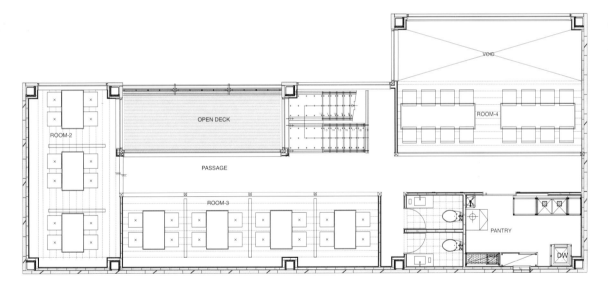

VOID

ROOM-2

OPEN DECK

PASSAGE

ROOM-3

ROOM-4

PANTRY

DW

Plan:
The RC building housing the restaurant is new, and contrasts dramatically with the retrospective atmosphere of the interior.

Scorpione
Toshiya Kobayashi
Gion, Kyoto

One hundred years have passed since this building, now housing the Italian restaurant, Scorpione, was built as an *ochaya*, in which *geisha* entertained guests with singing, dancing, and repartee. The building is located in Kyoto's Gion quarter, which is famous for its rows of *machiya* (terraced) houses.

The former owner had intended to tear down the building and erect something modern and easier to maintain, but designer Toshiya Kobayashi convinced him of the value of preserving the original structure. Kobayashi worked hard to come up with a design that left the original features in place where possible while he outfitted the space with a modern kitchen and other facilities.

The interior is divided into three sections: a *tatami*-mat area, a bar, and a Western-style dining room with tables and chairs. A small courtyard with an *ishidoro* (stone lantern) divides the three sections, and also provides a focal point.

The original *fusuma* (sliding doors made of paper) have been replaced with glass doors, making all three areas visible from the entrance. The ceiling boards have also been taken down to reveal the beams supporting the roof of the building; these elements and the glass doors combined contribute to the sense of spaciousness in the space. To offset these modern touches, the walls are plastered with mud mixed with straw, a traditional wall covering in Japan, and wooden grilles of the style associated with *machiya* buildings, are fitted into the windows.

In contrast to the traditional, Japanese appearance of the exterior and many of the interior fittings, the furniture represents a range of Asian styles. The wooden chairs ranged round the bar, for example, were made in the Philippines in the colonial style, while a leather-upholstered sofa in the waiting area complements a screen painted with birds and flowers to add a pan-Asian feel.

Together these elements combine to create an exotic mixture of old and new, domestic and foreign.

Opposite:
At the counter bar on the ground floor, Spanish style chairs sit with a Chinese-style table creating an international atmosphere.

Left:
The detached private room on the first floor has the original fittings, but the colorful and chic furniture has revitalized the overall atmosphere.

Plan:
The old two-storey wooden house is sandwiched between two modern buildings but it extends backwards a long way. The waiting lounge, bar counter, *tatami*-matted room and kitchen are on the ground floor, while on the first floor the general dining area and a *tatami*-matted room for private parties are connected by a corridor.

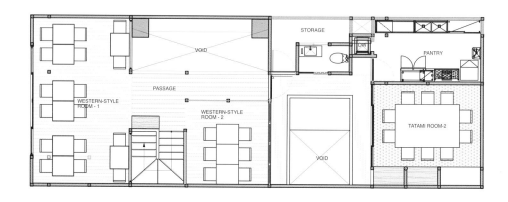

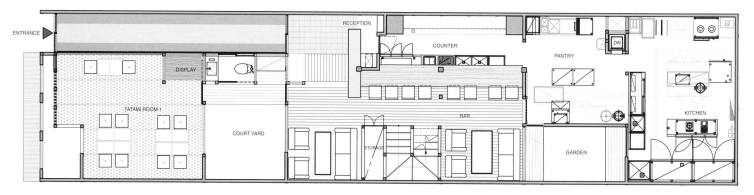

Kushi no Bou
Gen Yokoi
Shinjuku, Tokyo

Shinjuku is one of Tokyo's most fashionable shopping districts and famous for its many up-market department stores. Located in this area, Kushi no Bou offers *kushiage* dishes of meat and vegetables battered and deep-fried on skewers, attracting customers as much for the character of its design as for its tasty food.

The designer who was commissioned for this project, Gen Yokoi, was asked to make good use of his collection of antique handcrafted furniture, collected over a number of years from old Japanese country houses. To offset the dignified, slightly oppressive quality of this furniture, he also had in mind a space with a light and airy atmosphere.

The four main materials Yokoi has used are *aji* stone, bamboo, earth, and *washi* (handmade paper), which are all very traditional. However, he has treated these elements in new ways in order to create a contemporary nuance. The ceiling, for example, is covered with thinly split and delicately knitted bamboo nets that hide the lighting, so that the room is illuminated more softly. Through the *washi*, the light fills the room with subtle illumination and shadow. The walls covered with earth, using a traditional technique, provide sophisticated texture within the space.

The one element that ties together the different materials and objects in this space are the thick old beams originating from the roof of an old Japanese farmhouse, which have been used here in a distinctly modern way.

The *hikarikabe* (illuminated wall) is made from *washi*, and when lit from the back creates interesting shadows throughout the room.

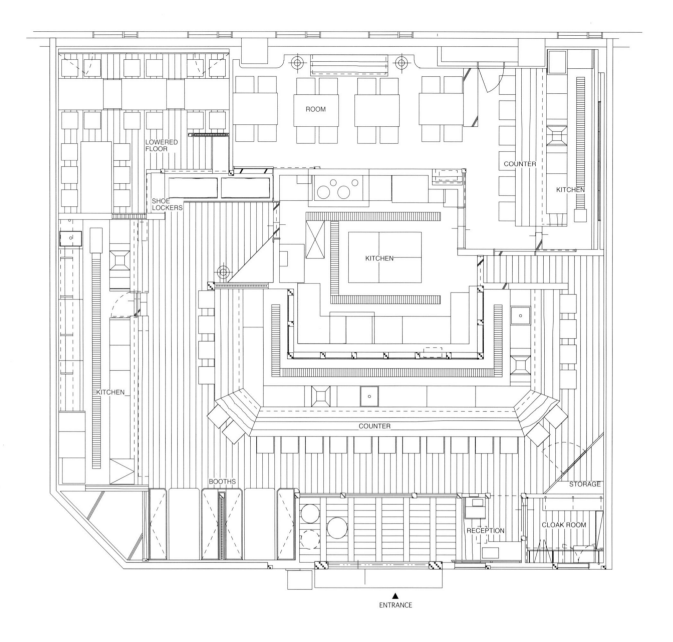

ROOM

LOWERED
FLOOR

SHOE
LOCKERS

KITCHEN

COUNTER

KITCHEN

KITCHEN

COUNTER

BOOTHS

STORAGE

RECEPTION

CLOAK ROOM

▲
ENTRANCE

Plan:
Kushi no Bou offers *kushi-age*, split-fried vegetables and meats, very popular in Japan, and the restaurant is always crowded with people of all ages.

Above:
A stone fountain sits beside the drinks counter.

Right:
The thick beams running across the ceiling were taken from an old farmhouse.

Kichiri
Yukimasa Numata
Minami-Honmachi, Osaka

This sophisticated Japanese restaurant is located on the edge of one of Osaka's most bustling areas, and is always crowded with young businesspeople who drop by after their work day. The understated entrance consists of steps leading up to the restaurant, flanked by white pillars.

A narrow passage from the entrance to the main dining room is dimly lit by unique light fixtures in the shape of wine buckets, and it is reminiscent of the kind of rustic path that leads to a typical teahouse. "I paid a lot of attention to the ambience of the area between the entrance and the dining area," the designer, Yukimasa Numata, says. "Guests walk through a relatively dimly lit passage and suddenly find themselves in a brighter space full of life, which I hope has the effect of creating a feeling of drama." At the end of the passage, pieces of bamboo painted in white are pasted on the wall.

Numata has adopted bamboo as a design motif. The pillars at the entrance feature stencils designed to resemble bamboo slats, and this same pattern appears on the partition boards in the main dining room. The restaurant's dining tables are made of pressed bamboo boards.

The dining room is divided into a main dining area, an area of banquettes, and rooms for private parties. The light fixtures in the main dining area consist of *washi* (handmade paper) and wood and resemble traditional Japanese lamps.

Modern materials are also used to offset these more traditional features, including a wall covered in padded white leather. The other walls are covered with tiles, the irregular surface of which provide a sense of depth. A bar made of ceramic and glass tiles has the appearance of a fireplace in a Western home.

Unity is added by a color scheme consisting of only ivory and mahogany, while the simple, clean overall design provides a convival atmosphere.

Opposite:
In this private room for parties, the textured earth walls and *tokonoma* (recessed alcove) are balanced with the more contemporary style of the thick cushions and limited color scheme.

Left:
Bamboo is the main motif in this restaurant design, but Numata makes moderate use of it on the white partitions in the dining room. The spaces created behind the partitions give guests privacy while still staying open to the dining room.

Plan:
Wooden panels and latticework separate the banquettes from the main dining room.

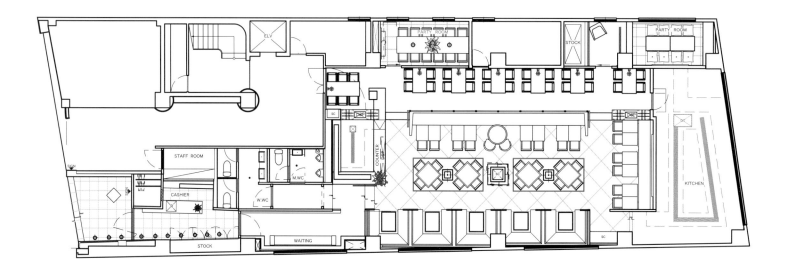

Part 3
Cultural Cohesion

The combination of elements of traditional Japanese design with motifs and items borrowed from outside the country — especially from other parts of Asia — leads to eclectic, hybrid restaurants with an Asia-wide appeal. These designs offer such unique combinations as antique European lampshades and *tatami*-matted walls; faux rice fields set against Western furniture and photographs; as well as wall surfaces covered with Chinese prints and mirrors. Bringing together features from a variety of cultures adds variety and a sense of playfulness, creating very attractive dining environments.

Ken's Dining
Yasumichi Morita
Shinjuku, Tokyo

The area around Tokyo's Shinjuku station is one of the busiest in the city. A clutch of high-rises to the west of the station houses some of the capital's most famous corporate names, but few truly stylish dining spots. According to designer Yasumichi Morita, "This area had no restaurants where diners might feel appropriately dressed in their Chanel or Armani suits. I wanted to create one."

The result is Ken's Dining, a delicatessan-style cafe-restaurant located on the ground and basement floors of an office building. The deli-style counter on the ground floor has a long row of seats lined up alongside, with a wall of mirrors behind it that opens up the space. Photos of farmers and fishermen going about their work in various parts of Asia are a key design element in this area.

Downstairs the mood is different, as there is a considerably larger space, in which the centerpiece is a huge table of almost 30 square meters (323 sq ft) in size. This is highlighted by two huge light fixtures standing more than two and a half meters (8 ft) high, with cloth lampshades for which Morii gained inspiration from the thatched roofs of old farmhouses. The table serves a practical as well as aesthetic purpose, as it makes it easier for the waiters to serve the diners than if the room were cluttered with a number of smaller tables. The walls flanking the staircase to this area are covered in *tatami* (woven straw) mats — usually used as a flooring material — while illumination is provided in by lights in antique lampshades.

Overleaf:
The golden room at Daidaiya, Ginza. A gold *washi* pasted wall reveals a digital patterned image when illuminated from behind. Designer Hashimoto incorporated some typical Japanese elements in this original, avant-garde design.

Right:
The main dining room at Ken's Dining is underground, with mirrors in the ceiling and walls combining with the wooden latticework to create a dramatic effect. Between the mirrors Chinese antique engravings are mounted and lit from below.

One of the walls in the basement area is decorated with *tenkoku* (engraved) lithographs in a traditional Chinese style, and another is decorated with mirrors and light bars, both of which provide the illusion of spaciousness.

Morii has fused a variety of cultural elements here, from Chinese antique seal-engraving to European-style furniture to Japanese lampshades, producing a dramatic but coherent whole. The ingenious use of mirrors and illumination add an air of mystique. The skilful lighting technique obscures surrounding tables, drawing the guests' attention to their own dishes and conversation.

Opposite:
Strategically-placed mirrors and lighting enhance the impression of the Chinese seal engravings on the back wall.

Plan:
The take-out deli and café, with its 20 seats on the ground floor, attracts young people with its casual atmosphere in this, one of the busiest areas of Tokyo. Underground, the chic restaurant serves a fashionable crowd who comes to enjoy the chef's original dishes based on Asian ingredients. A key feature is the large table situated in the center of the room.

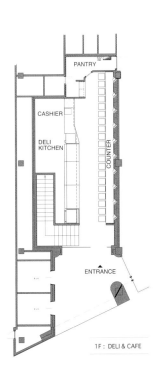

1F : DELI & CAFE

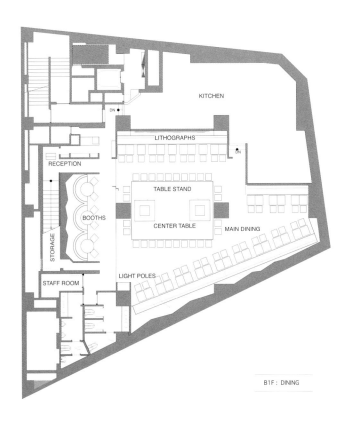

B1F : DINING

Left:
Another feature of the restaurant are the two large lampshades positioned on the central table. Their shape resembles the thatched roof of an old Japanese farmhouse.

Opposite:
The walls of the stairway to the basement restaurant are covered with *tatami* mats, the borders of which form patterns which reflect the latticework in the restaurant. The combination of the wall mounted mats and the large lampshade is striking.

Right:
Designer Morita has paid close attention to lighting, adjusting light and shadow to show off the dishes, and the guests, more attractively. The chairs are designed to match the color and style of the space.

Left:
Above the deli showcase, photographs of locations around Asian countries line the wall.

Murata Mitsui
Yasumichi Morita
Minami-Honmachi, Osaka

Right:
The walls of the main dining
room are covered with
square cypress wood *sake*
measures. Combined with
the clever use of lights
and mirrors, this creates an
impressive effect.

Below left:
On the façade of the restaurant, *kawara* are set in the
white stucco painted wall
and lit from the top.

This restaurant, which is named after the owner,
is located in an old, two-storey wooden house in the
center of Osaka. Murata Mitsui presented designer
Yasumichi Morita with the challenge of creating
a casual *izakaya* (Japanese tapas bar) tavern in the
space within a limited budget.

As the small house is overshadowed by the high
buildings it stands between, Morita was prompted
to design a façade that attracts the attention
of passers-by. This took the form of a white stucco
surface entirely studded, in regular rows running
from top to bottom, with slate grey *kawara* (roof tiles).
In the evening hours, when the façade is illuminated
by blue light, it acts as a beacon, drawing the
attention of those passing.

Inside the 36-seat dining room, two walls are
covered with the square cedar *masu* (*sake* measures) in which *sake* is sometimes served. These
vessels were presented to the owner by a number
of *sake* brewers. The effect of some 3,500 square
cups lining the walls is dramatic, and set off by the
mirrors set on the adjacent walls.

A small room set with *tatami*-mat floors is available for private parties of six to seven people.
The walls in this room are covered with corrugated
plastic sheets, lit from behind. Decorative cords
have been woven through their surface.

Though the design of both the interior and exterior of this restaurant is bold, the mood overall is a
comfortable, relaxed one that reflects the personality
of the owner.

Three thousand *sake* measures were use to create the unique atmosphere in this small Japanese restaurant.

A touch of humor in the bathroom, with the use of a water fountain, of the kind found in Japanese public parks, and naked light bulbs hanging from the ceiling.

The restaurant is on the first floor of a small, old house that has been refurbished. It is surrounded by tall modern buildings in the midst of the bustling streets of Osaka. The main dining room with counter seating is near the entrance, with a private dining room further back. As the restaurant is very small, designer Morita made good use of mirrors to make it feel more spacious.

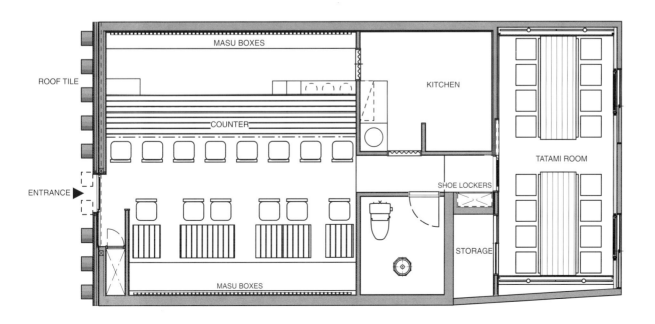

ROOF TILE

ENTRANCE

MASU BOXES

COUNTER

MASU BOXES

KITCHEN

SHOE LOCKERS

STORAGE

TATAMI ROOM

The wall of this private room is covered with corrugated plastic sheets tied together with fabric and lit from behind.

Niu

Yasumichi Morita
Aoyama, Tokyo

Opposite:
This interesting decoration on the wall is created by passing fabric through small holes in transparent acrylic board. The pink illumination suggests the color of a lotus flower.

Below left:
In the main dining room, two rows of standing floor lamps with yellow lotus flower shades are arranged along the passageway.

This Chinese restaurant is innovatively designed, with a lotus flower motif, contributing to the sense of unity. The three colors related to the lotus — the bright pink of the flower, the striking yellow of the flower when still in bud, and the pea green of the leaf — are used throughout the space.

An ornate door, prominent wine cellar, and lotus plants floating in a small antique ceramic vessel greet guests as they descend the staircase from the street-level entrance to the restaurant located in the basement of a modern building.

In the bar area, a back-lit green wall featuring a cut-out dragon design makes a dramatic backdrop, while standard lamps shaped to resemble lotuses are dotted about the dining area.

The main dining room is divided into two sections, with counter seating occupying one area and tables and chairs the other. Along the main wall are mounted panels lit from behind in pink, providing a soft ambience in the dining area. The panels consist of a mirrored back and glass front sandwiching transparent plastic sheets which are held together by the cords woven vertically through them.

Designer Yasumichi Morita regards lighting as the most important element in the design of a restaurant. "Diffused lighting combined with more precisely directed spotlights provide a feeling of depth. The walls of the restaurant are lit from below, producing a three-dimensional effect as objects reflect off the mirror surface built into the wall," he explains.

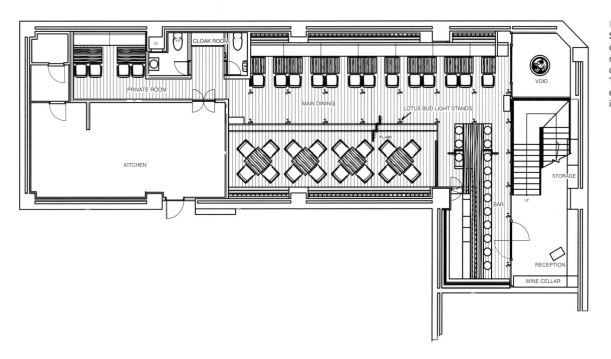

Contrast is also provided by the yellow lighting of the lotus standard lamps and the pink glow of the wall.

This highly original design has attracted much attention and helped to make this restaurant one of Tokyo's more popular new venues.

Delicate screens in which partially translucent fabric is sandwiched between two pieces of glass are placed between the tables. "The diffused lighting and the screens produce a relaxed atmosphere in which diners can concentrate on the food, the wine and the conversation without being distracted," explains Ohashi.

Opposite:
The wall behind the bar beside the entrance is a backlit green glass with a large graphic of a dragon.

Right:
The fabric weave, a prominent motif within the restaurant, dominates the large entrance door.

Africa
Yasumichi Morita
Daikanyama, Tokyo

Daikanyama is one of Tokyo's trendiest shopping districts and is bountifully supplied with boutiques and restaurants. Africa, located in the area, is a restaurant that has gained a following with diners who enjoy eating good food in a striking setting.

The design of the restaurant, despite its name, incorporates elements not only from Africa but also from Bali, Italy, France, and Japan.

The 330 square meter (3,552 sq ft) space is large enough for displaying a variety of ornaments, selected by designer Yoshiyuki Morii. As guests pass from the bistro, nearest the entrance, to the bar, they move from a casual environment to a more chic and formal atmosphere.

The different sections of the restaurant are made distinct through variation in lighting and the use of partitions. The bistro is illuminated by sunlight streaming in through large windows during daylight hours; Morita's lighting ensures it remains brightly lit in the evening. In the bar and dining areas, the lighting is, in contrast, dimmer and more intimate.

The ceiling of the dining area is painted black and the tables are individually highlighted with overhead spotlights. This is intended to provide the illusion of dining under the night sky of the African savannah or within the Balinese jungle. In the bar section, lighting is provided only by candles positioned randomly throughout the space.

Large partitions of one and a half meters (4.9 ft) in height and more than two meters (6.6 ft) in width are used not only to divide up each section, but as

Large Africa-inspired artworks are framed and used as division partitions between the dining section and the bar. Balinese earthenware pots are scattered throughout the space along with other ornaments in a mixture of African and Asian styles. In contrast the food is Italian and French.

Above:
The ceiling of the dining and bar area is painted black to provide guests with a feeling of 'being in the Savannah.' The lighting and pots are from Bali. The etched glass separates the bar from the dining room.

Right:
Along the corridor leading from the entrance to the dining room, African and Asian style ornaments can be seen in a long display case.

Far right:
The large blackboard in the more casual café section besides the entrance shows the day's menu.

Plan:
The restaurant looks out on to a courtyard and light flow through the large glass window into the café area besides the entrance, while the dining and bar areas are more dimly lit.

a key design element containing paintings of African women and exotic plants by a Swedish artist, Heidi Lange. The focal point of the bistro is a huge blackboard, on which the menu is written.

Morii, who was brought up in an old *kimono* merchant's house in Kyoto, referenced the partitioned layout of his one-time residence in his design for Africa. "Even though the floor space overall is considerable, I divided up the space with partitions and various objects in order to provide a more intimate feeling in which Japanese guests would feel comfortable. The Japanese have a different sense of space than do people who are accustomed to living in more expansive lands and would not necessarily feel comfortable dining in a large room with high ceilings," says Morii. The large partitions are more than simple decorations. Their size and positioning is calculated to give a stronger impression than a regular wall, without an imposing, oppressive presence.

Whether many people would agree with these ideas or not, they would concur that Morii has designed a restaurant that effectively combines drama with intimacy in a unique way.

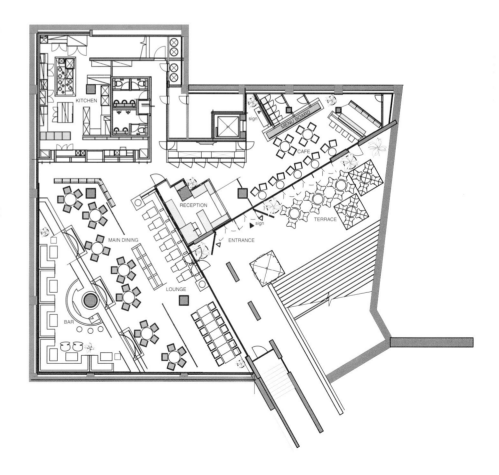

Tile
Yoshiyuki Morii
Horie, Osaka

The dried rice plants set in the middle of the counter add to the rustic atmosphere of this Korean restaurant. The designer saw in the rice plants a symbol of Southeast Asia, which would stimulate not only a feeling of nostalgia in the guests but also vitality.

Horie, an area located in the suburbs of Osaka about ten minutes from the center of the city by train, has prospered since the 16th century as a distribution center because of its canal system lined with warehouses. With rents in the area considerably cheaper than those in the center of the city, many artists and designers have set up establishments here, and this has helped turn the area into a stylish district attracting many fashionable restaurants and cafes.

Designer Yoshiyuki Morii describes that area as being "like New York's Soho, having attracted young artists who set up studios in the old warehouses."

Tile is a thriving Korean restaurant in the area and is named after the fact that it is located in what was once a tile manufacturer's warehouse. The focal point of the interior is a faux rice field, planted with rows of dried rice stalks and surrounded by an oval counter 30 meters (98 ft) in length.

The inspiration for this rice field came on a trip to Bali, Morii says. "I had lunch once in a spot overlooking a rice field, and thought that probably only Southeast Asian people could see the true beauty in that kind of scenery. I wanted to create something of this experience for diners at Tile," he says.

Morii was given a limited budget to work with, which encouraged him to leave many of the existing fittings in place and select used furniture for use within the restaurant. The design is appropriate to the building and highlights the warehouse's original features.

Right:
The restaurant is situated in an area of the city where once many warehouses stood. Now redeveloped, the area is crowded with young people who enjoy shopping and dining in the new, fashionable boutiques and restaurants.

Left:
The limited budget prevented designer Morii from carrying out an extensive renovation of this old tile warehouse. The walls were painted in white and the ceiling remains untouched, adding to the casual mood of the space.

Opposite:
On the first floor beside the stairway, a box with dried green rice plants is illuminated from above and sits next to an Asian antique chest.

Right:
Decorating the first floor
are pictures by New York
photographer Nigel Scott.
Second hand chairs
and tables fill the space.

Opposite:
The first floor space is also
filled with used furniture
collected from various
second-hand shops. The
letter shapes from used
signboards are an interesting
element in the high ceiling.

Plan:
Situated within a converted
warehouse, the Korean
restaurant has a 30m²
(323 ft²) counter on the
ground floor.

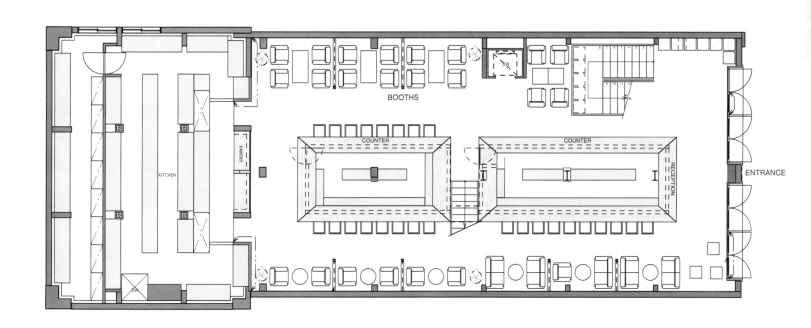

Daidaiya Ginza
Yukio Hashimoto
Ginza, Tokyo

Passing through the 60 meter (197 ft) long passage that runs from the entrance of this restaurant to the interior, guests can admire designer Yukio Hashimoto's selection of several beautiful antique Japanese objects.

At the entrance, a pair of white cones of sand welcomes guests. These *tatesuna* are symbolic of the spirits inhabiting the mountains and have long had a place at the entrance to Shinto shrines. The designer chose to place them at the entrance to the restaurant not so much because of their meaning as because he is "fascinated by their form and color."

Along both sides of the long passage, bare light bulbs provide illumination, an idea the designer took from a festival held nearby, where stalls lining the streets are lit by strings of exposed bulbs. "I know the history of each design element, but I do not want to be tied to tradition," Hashimoto insists. "What I try to do is to express my idea of Japan."

Laying gold foil on wall and ceiling surfaces is a traditional feature of Japanese design and is meant to give a sense of the scenery of nirvana. In Daidaiya, gold foil covers the walls and ceilings of small private rooms, providing a feel that is both luxurious and traditional.

A performance stage is situated in the middle of the restaurant. Its backdrop consists of an abstract design in the Japanese *rimpa* style (black ink on gold paper). Even the restaurant itself is a stage on which traditional Japan elements are displayed for modern diners; this intention gives the area a feeling of drama.

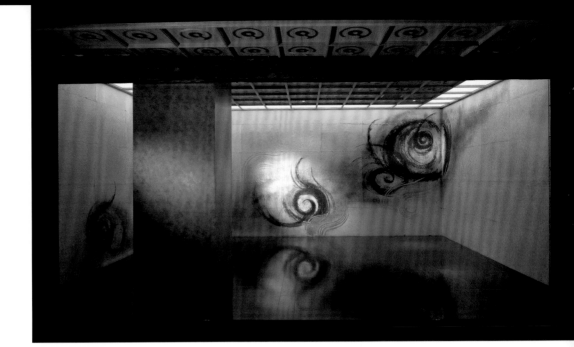

Opposite:
An unexpected design combining swords with *kimono* sashes greet guests as they enter this dining room.

Right:
A small space similar to a Noh stage is situated near the entrance and used for performances and live events. The backdrop is an original painting by a Japanese artist.

Left:
The walls, the ceiling, and the table of this private dining room are covered with gold foil.

Left:
Above the long counter, images of flowers printed on liquid crystal film and set in glass provide a dramatic effect.

Plan:
A variety of impressive spaces lead off the 60 meters (197 ft) long corridor like a festival at a shrine. Each section, from the counter, the hall way, the large dining room to the private dining rooms have been designed differently and guests can appreciate the variety of atmospheres by just walking up and down the passageway.

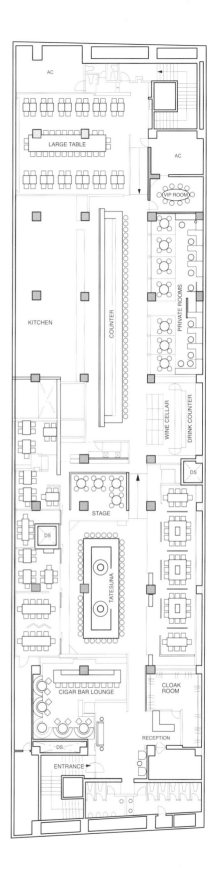

Lee Nang Ha
Toshio Koyama
Daikanyama, Tokyo

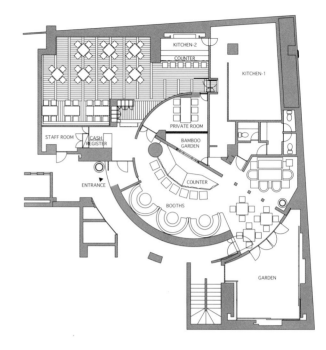

Above:
Situated on the ground floor in the fashionable Daikanyama district of Tokyo, the restaurant is recognizable as Korean just by the curved wall covered with earth and antique stone objet besides the entrance.

Plan:
The restaurant is divided into two differerently-styled parts: one is Korean; the other is more western in style but is decorated with Asian and Japanese antique ornaments.

Elegant Korean cuisine is served in this sophisticated restaurant, which is named after the owner. Designer Toshio Koyama was given the task of expressing the notion of yin and yang, the balance between two forces of opposite nature, in the restaurant design.

Koyama met this challenge by emphasizing contrast wherever possible: bright lighting with dimmer areas; antique items with modern furniture; and the rough texture of the walls with the smooth floor.

The restaurant is divided into two sections, one of which consists of a raised area in the traditional Korean *ondol* (heated wooden flooring) style. The walls and ceiling are plastered with diatomite earth, which controls the humidity and helps to keep the temperature of the room even. Wooden boards taken from an American barn are used in partitions that divide up the space. The rustic surface of these boards contrasts with the elaborate antique Korean furniture used in the restaurant.

In the other dining area, where guests remove their shoes before entering, lights with shades from Edo *kiriko* cut glass (made in vivid colors typical of the Edo era) are featured. This glass has been produced in the Tokyo area since the 17th century. The beautiful colors and sparkle produced by these lights add a charming touch to the otherwise dimly lit area. Other design elements found in this restaurant include antique Korean furniture, Japanese ceramics, and glassware.

Lee Nang Ha mixes various cultural elements into a coherent and attractive whole.

The western style room is filled with antique ornaments and original design earthenware pots. Lights with Edo *kiriko* glass shades are placed on pieces of antique agricultural machinery to the back of the room.

In a small recessed room beside the entrance to the Korean style section, dishes are prepared and served at a counter. Silhouettes of Korean style earthenware pots can be seen on the illuminated shelves.

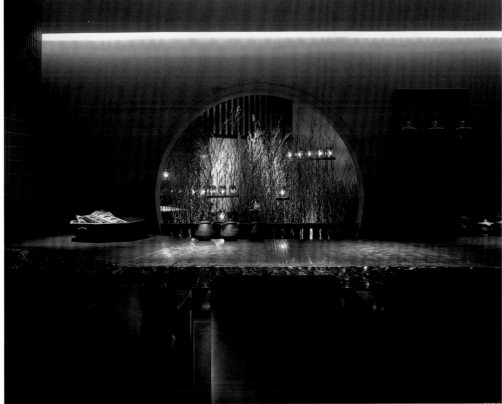

In the raised floor Korean-style section of the restaurant, the low tables and antique Korean chests are illuminated both by spotlights in the ceiling and by hidden lights in the floor. The walls are covered with diatomite earth.

Futong Mandarin

Toshiya Kobayashi
Marunouchi, Tokyo

Opposite:
This raised wooden pathway above a stone floor leads guests to the dining room. The kitchen is set to the right side of the corridor, while the dining space is to the left.

Below:
The Chinese restaurant is situated in the ground floor of an old-fashioned office building constructed in 1964. The silver metallic signboard displaying the name of the restaurant in Chinese character catches one's eye in this upmarket business area.

This Chinese restaurant is located on the ground floor of an office building constructed in 1964 in Marunouchi, a busy business district in central Tokyo. The solemn look of the building gives this contemporary restaurant a dignified air, which explains its popularity with local business people, who congregate here after their work hours.

The designer focused on "minimalism with a Japanese taste" in the entrance area, which features glass and steel in a design that is reminiscent of a Mondrian painting. In fact, one might for moment wonder if this is indeed a Chinese restaurant. The wall and floor here are laid with whitish stones with a silver glint; a wooden platform set a few centimeters (1–2 in) above this stone floor leads guests to the dining area and bar.

The corridor is positioned between the dining space and the kitchen area, which can be seen through large plates of glass. At the end of the corridor, a large post adorned with a Chinese poem indicates the direction of the main dining area and the bar.

The main dining area features a central pillar decorated with paintings of banana trees, accentuating the exotic Asian feel of the establishment. The wall behind the bar is covered with antique Chinese chests originally used to hold potions at a chemist's shop, with the drawers now holding bottles of alcoholic elixir of various kinds.

The Chinese atmosphere is accentuated by such features as antique lampshades and Chinese characters brushed on some of the pillars found throughout the restaurant. These elements are offset with simple furniture and fittings in a modern, Western style.

Overall, the atmosphere in Futong Mandarin is one of pan-Asian flair combined with sleek and modern elements.

Above:
A banana leaf is painted on this central pillar contributing to the atmosphere of Asian resort.

Left:
In this small dining room for private parties, the relaxing sofas and table are inspired by Chinese design.

Plan:
The L-shape structure of the restaurant makes it possible to incorporate different design styles in the section near the entrance and a more secluded rear area. Designer Kobayashi used different types of lighting and furniture in each area. Late in the evening the area at the rear of the restautant is transformed into the bar.

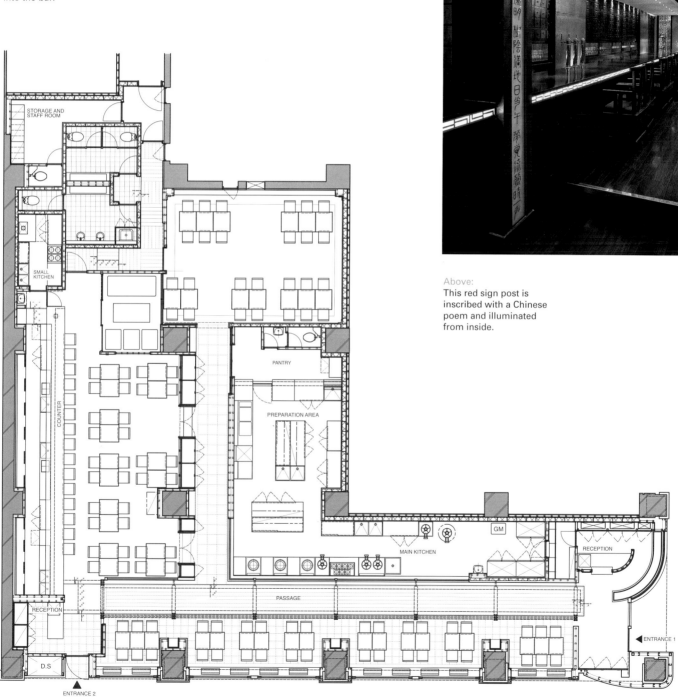

STORAGE AND STAFF ROOM

SMALL KITCHEN

COUNTER

PANTRY

PREPARATION AREA

MAIN KITCHEN

GM

RECEPTION

RECEPTION

PASSAGE

ENTRANCE 1

D.S

ENTRANCE 2

Above:
This red sign post is inscribed with a Chinese poem and illuminated from inside.

Kamonka
Yukio Hashimoto
Ginza, Tokyo

This Chinese restaurant is named after an old Chinese myth about a house from which emanated such enticing smells of cooking food that passers-by would have to stop, unable to go any further.

Designer Yuki Ohhashimoto was asked to combine traditional and modern elements to create an unclichéd interior.

"The owner asked me to create a restaurant of a kind not seen before," he says. Hashimoto visited Shanghai and other parts of China for inspiration and decór items. He was most impressed with Shanghai's Yuen Park, a busy amusement area in which taverns and souvenir shops stand on both sides of the narrow streets. Thus he has attempted to reproduce the feeling of this neighborhood in the Kamonka restaurant.

Partitions with ornamental carving are positioned between the tables in the dining area; both these dividers and the tables and chairs were purchased during Hashimoto's travels in China.

Wishing to avoid a typical old Chinese atmosphere, the designer has added touches like stainless steel frames for the partitions. Sleek modern lampshades provide a contrast to the antique furniture. "Mixing strongly Chinese elements and sleek contemporary materials creates an exotic atmosphere," he suggests.

"This is a Chinese restaurant, but the fundamental components are all of an original design. The challenge was in finding the right balance between original and more traditional elements," says Hashimoto.

Below:
Beside the entrance door of the restaurant, Chinese characters are written on a glass window, behind which is a humorous Chinese antique stone sculpture.

The round tables, beams, pillars, and walls are painted in rich red lacquer. The dining room can be divided by sliding doors.

Above:
Private dining rooms, the antique ornamental wooden carvings are set between stainless steel covered pillars. The wooden lattice-work and partitions over the doors are also Chinese antique. This combination of old and new materials creates a dynamic atmosphere.

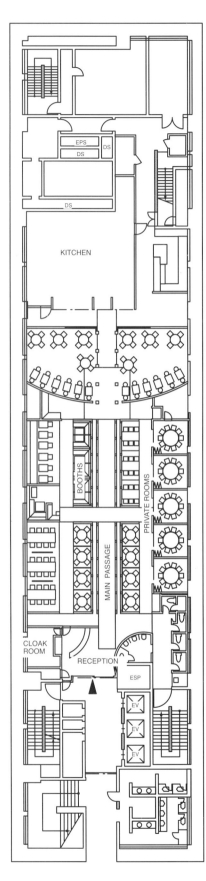

Plan:
Situated on a single floor, this long and narrow Chinese restaurant is divided into two parts by the straight corridor stretching from the entrance to its far end. Along both sides of the corridor dining areas are situated with private dining rooms set along the walls. The designer arranged antique furniture and fittings, collected in Mainland China to his specification, to create a luxurious and mysterious atmosphere.

Right:
Illuminated poles stand in rows along the main corridor. The interesting pattern on the poles, made of acrylic resin, has been taken from that found on a Chinese antique wooden partition.

Epilogue
I Love Restaurants

by Ichiro Sato

Restaurant design is a field in which more latitude is allowed to the designer than is provided within the constraints of traditional architecture. Contemporary restaurant design reflects the tastes of ordinary people and builds on the aesthetic history of the particular country. In discussing contemporary restaurant design in Japan, it is necessary first to review the history of restaurants and their design in this country.

Restaurants in Japan date back to the end of the Muromachi era (1331–1598), when establishments called *chaya*, literally "tea shops," served pilgrims on their way to or from temples and shrines. These *chaya* were generally simple affairs, with benches set out for customers to enjoy tea and sweets or locally produced food.

In the Edo era (1590–1868), these establishments became more substantial and began to specialize in particular types of food or drink. It was during this period that *izakaya* taverns (Japanese tapas bars), traditional pubs, noodle shops, and high-class restaurants began to appear.

The Westernization that swept Japan after the shift of power from the shoguns back to the emperor in the late nineteenth century spurred the establishment of new types of restaurants serving both Western-style food and more conventional Japanese dishes. During the Meiji period (1868–1912), fascination with all things foreign, particularly Western, and a desire to keep up with the latest fashion and culinary tastes brought change to dietary habits. Beef and dairy products were introduced to the Japanese palate at this time.

The first Western-style coffee shop opened in 1888 in Tokyo's Ginza area, and similar establishments were soon popping up around the city. A style of cooking combining Western ingredients and Japanese cooking techniques known as *yoshoku* (*yo* meaning Western, and *shoku* referring to food) developed in the early twentieth century, and every one of the fashionable department stores that were by this time popular attractions in themselves housed at least one *yoshoku* restaurant.

Japan has long been known for taking foreign inspiration for food, fashion, and other elements of culture and combining it with native elements to create a new amalgam that is, in the end, uniquely Japanese. This is evident in the way Japanese can comfortably adhere to both the native Shinto religion and the imported Buddhist creed. More recently, elements of Christianity have also crept in through wedding ceremonies and major festivals. This fusion of diverse elements may sometimes seem fickle or chaotic, but it is a great source of innovation.

The Japanese food service industry went through dramatic changes after World War II. Kyoto was spared the air raids, leaving its historic buildings intact. Tokyo, in contrast, was almost completely destroyed. A period of rapid post-war reconstruction created much of the capital we see today.

It took less than two decades from the end of World War II for various styles of restaurants, from

Tawaraya is a luxurious
restaurant and inn situated
in Kyoto. Founded some
300 years ago, it is one of
Japan's oldest and of a style
popular since the Edo era.
This traditional design has
become a model for many
of today's contemporary
restaurant design.

elegant and gorgeous French restaurants to fast
food shops, to boom in the big cities of Japan. The
major fast food chains such as McDonald's and
Kentucky Fried Chicken opened their first shops in
1970, to immediate success among the young. As
the variety of food on the Japanese table expanded,
the style of restaurant design varied. After the austere
years during and after the war, Japanese restaurant-
goers became interested not only in the food but
in the atmosphere and design of the eatery. Young
people attached greater importance where to
eat than what to eat when they chose restaurants.
Kitsch design influenced by European and American
pop culture gained popularity in coffee shops and
Italian restaurants. Casual noodle shops or *izakaya*,
on the other hand, continued to attract people with
their traditional Japanese design. The variety of
styles in the Japanese food service industry have
been expanding rapidly since the 1970s.

Those born in the years leading up to and soon
after 1960 have been labeled the "new generation."
This generation is sandwiched between two baby
booms: 1945 to 1950, and 1975 to 1980. Those
born during these booms are marked by a competi-
tiveness typical of large peer groups, whereas those
belonging to the new generation are more likely to
be motivated by a desire to find a balance between
opposing views than to see their personal views
emerge victorious.

The first set of baby boomers has been marked
by a fascination with the West — particularly

America. This generation introduced many of the
post-war fashion, music, and lifestyle trends,
as well as launching movements of rebellion and
new political thought. In architecture, interior
design, fashion, and the food-service industry, a
succession of eminent talents appeared during the
1960s and 1970s. It is fair to say that this first
set of boomers set the pattern for modern urban
life in Japan.

In the area of restaurant design, the first baby
boomers pioneered new forms and styles, presenting
the new generation with the challenge of building
on this achievement whilst still creating something
uniquely our own. One of the characteristics of
this new generation is its information sensibility,
developed from years of exposure to radio, television
and other media. More recently, the Internet and
satellite broadcasting has given us even greater
access to information on trends around the world.
We can see images of a restaurant just opened
in New York or London within minutes of the ribbon-
cutting, giving us an idea of the latest global developments with a speed and thoroughness of which
our predecessors could only have dreamed.

Along with this access to information, we have
also seen a broadening of interest in foreign soci-
eties. While the focus of attention was once almost
exclusively on America and Europe, a broadening
of tourism destinations has given us a familiarity
with the culture of East Asia, the Middle East, Africa,
and South America.

This has, in turn, influenced restaurant design. We are now just as likely to aim at conjuring the atmosphere of a Southeast Asian resort or a Chinese village as we are the ambience of a French bistro or Italian café. It is the skill of the new generation to be able to balance these different cultural elements thanks to our ability to filter information. For us, the Japanese tradition is one of diversity in which we feel free to combine new elements with conventional materials and techniques to create something never before seen.

Just as important as taking inspiration from both the Japanese vernacular and foreign styles is the task of creating unique designs that offer a comfortable atmosphere for the diner while saying something about modern life.

Each restaurant must be a unique experience for the diner, and it is the designer's job to find a way to express what a restaurant is about. This involves considering fundamental elements such as location, budget, clientele, and contemporary style. A restaurant's design should convince both diners and staff that this restaurant has to exist at this spot, at this time. In other words, a restaurant should give the impression that if it did not exist it would have to be invented.

For me, the best way to ensure that the design of a restaurant is original and successful is to decide on a core around which the design can take shape. This core can be a material, an item of décor or even a unique service of the restaurant. Every element of

the design should in some way refer to this core in a way that allows the restaurant to tell a kind of story to diners.

As an example of the kind of challenges designers face, I was asked to design a space where guests could enjoy something similar to a traditional tea ceremony but with a casual overall feel. In the tea ceremony host and guests collaborate; tea is prepared and served in front of the guests while they take an active interest in the tools and crockery. In a traditional tea ceremony there is little distance between guests and host. This was difficult to reproduce in a restaurant, where practicality demands some distance between customers and chef. This encouraged me to think of the counter between the chef and diners as being the core design element, allowing as it does for comfortable interaction between the kitchen and dining area while still providing a reasonable division between the two.

In designing the restaurant, I thought about what the guest would encounter upon entering. I envisioned a warm welcome from the chef and other kitchen staff as soon as a guest entered, after which the customer would be guided to a stool made of the same material as the counter, where he would be given a hot towel and something to drink. The guest would look over the counter and ask about dishes available that day, with the chef making recommendations according to season and the preferences of the guest. Choosing a core element in this way and imagining how the restaurant would

Wakuden, a century-old
restaurant, is situated in
northern Kyoto. Famous
for its top-class food, the
restaurant also offers stylish
interiors and a scenic
garden. Many elements of
its traditional design have
inspired the top designers
of today.

work as I was laying out the design allowed me to
create a space successful for both diners and
staff. At a restaurant serving Japanese cuisine, the
originality of the design might best be expressed by
using traditional materials in an innovative way. The
traditions of Japanese cuisine should also be taken
into account to create successful designs. In sushi
restaurants attention is focused on the chefs behind
the bar as they deftly slice fish and form rice into
small nuggets. In a traditional *kaiseki* restaurant
guests often spend several hours enjoying the small
dishes of seasonal delicacies that are served in a
tatami-mat room, often overlooking a garden or
scene of natural beauty. These traditions have long
influenced Japanese restaurant design.

A designer is well served by considerable experience of the way in which restaurants work, as
another aspect of successful design is practicality.
Designs that allow staff to function efficiently take
considerable thought and experience.

Many of us have eaten our most memorable
meals far from a conventional restaurant — at a
street-side stall or on a picnic blanket in the park.
And so a designer need not be confined by rigorous
ideas of what constitutes a stylish restaurant but
should be open to new ideas and ready to adapt to
the needs of a given project.

Japanese restaurant design is constantly devel-
oping and attracting increasing international attention. It is the new generation of designers that is
most responsible for today's innovative designs.

Designers

Yukio Hashimoto
Born: 1962
Designer; Chief Designer of Hashimoto Yukio Design Studio Co. Ltd; Lecturer at The Women's College of Fine Arts, Women's University of Fine Arts, and Aichi Prefectural University of Arts.
Main projects include: Daidaiya Ginza, Hika, Kamonka, La So, Toraji, Tsukino Shizuku.
4-2-5, Sendagaya, Shibuya-ku, Tokyo
Tel: 03-5474-1724; fax: 03-5474-4724
Email: hydesign@din.or.jp
http://www.din.or.jp/~hydesign/

Toshiya Kobayashi
Born: 1964
Space Designer; Art Director of First Kiwa Planning Co. Ltd.
Main projects include: Futong Mandarin, Shanghai Bar, Scorpione, Negiya Heikichi, Guinyo Guinyo, Casablanca Silk.
3F Chitose BLD, 2-22-8, Ohhashi, Meguro-ku, Tokyo
Tel: 03-5453-7791; fax: 03-5453-7793
Email: toshiya@kiwa-group.co.jp
http://www.kiwa-group.co.jp/

Ryu Kosaka
Born: 1960
Architect and Space Designer; Managing Director, design department of Nomura Co. Ltd (a commercial facilities design company).
Main projects include: Hanatei (Restaurant design 1st Prize of DDA), Torafuku, XEX, Rainbow Roll Sushi.
4-6-4,Shibaura, Minato-ku, Tokyo
Tel: 03-5476-1304; fax: 03-3451-7283
Email:ryuu_kosaka@nomurakougei.co.jp
http://www.retaildesign.jp/

Toshio Koyama
Born: 1958
Architect/Designer; President and Chief Designer of Swans ID Ltd.
Main projects include: Bishoku Shuka Chanto, Lee Nang Ha, ENOTORIA, Angelo Cafe.
#101 Twin Minami Aoyama, 3-14-13, Minami Aoyama, Minato-ku, Tokyo
Tel: 03-3405-5603; fax: 03-3478-5404
Email: swans-id@cd6.so-net.ne.jp

Yoshiyuki Morii
Born: 1967
Space designer; President of Cafe Co.
Main projects include: Africa, Shinobu Tei, Azool, Tile, Yakuchangu.
2F SIX BLDG, 2-11-13, Minami Horie, Nishi-ku, Osaka
Tel: 06-6533-8607; fax: 06-6533-8608
Email: morii@ca-fe.co.jp
http://www.ca-fe.co.jp/

Yasumichi Morita
Born: 1967
Architectural/ Interior/ Product/ Graphic Designer; C.E.O. and President of Glamorous Co. Ltd.
Main projects include: Murata Mitsui, Daidaiya (Shinsaibashi, Hong Kong, and others), Ken's Dining (Shinsai Bashi, Nishiazabu, Shinjuku), dai-sushi, Watami (Hong Kong), Niu.
3F, 1-14, Miyamae-cho, Nishinomiya City, Hyogo
Tel: 0798-33-5339; fax: 0798-33-6339
Email: ero-ero@glamorous.co.jp

Yukimasa Numata
Born: 1974
Architectural Space Designer; a representative of Numata Yukimasa Design Office.
Main projects include: Kichiri, Bisyokuka-Gochin, Sozaiya-Isuzu, Bellini.
3FNakajima BLD, 2-6-22,Minami-Honmachi, Chuo-ku, Osaka
Tel/fax: 06-6243-0505
Email: numata-design-office@soleil.ocn.ne.jp

Masaaki Ohashi
Born: 1943
Interior designer, representative of omdo Inc., member of Japanese society of commercial space designers, chairman of NT department at Toyo Art School
Main projects include: Bou's, Hana Noren (JCD design award, 1999), Chokyaku Yowa, Kushizo, Toho Kenbunroku.
Also an author of many books on restaurant planning and design.
#403 Toho Estate, 7-21-17, Roppongi, Minato-ku, Tokyo
Tel: 03-3479-4063; fax: 03-3479-4039
Email: ohhashi@sepia.ocn.ne.jp

Ichiro Sato
Born: 1962
Space Designer; a representative of age. Inc.
Main projects include: KAN, The River Oriental, Jiyugaoka Grill, The Hanezawa Garden on the Green at Hiroo, Tamasaka, Tuki no Niwa, The Tokyo Restaurant.
#102 Shoto Mansion, 2-29-8, Tomigaya Shibuya-ku, Tokyo
Tel: 03-5738-1031; fax: 03-5738-1032
Email: age-co@qf6.so-net.ne.jp

Fujio Takayama
Born: 1956
Architect; Space Designer; a
representative of Takayama Fujio
Design Associates.
Main projects include: Koomon (Lighting
awards 1996/ JCD design awards 1996),
San An (Lighting awards 1997/ JCD
design award 1997)
#305 Villa Hata, 6-33-1, Jingu Mae,
Shibuya-ku, Tokyo
Tel: 03-5467-3739; fax: 03-5467-3974
Email: design@takayamafujio.co.jp

Hisanobu Tsujimura
Born: 1961
Architect and Space Designer; a repre-
sentative of Moon Balance
Main projects include: DINING CAFE
RICORDI (14th The best of National
Lighting contests 1996), Cha Cha, Kiss of
Luminiscence, Bar Moon, Dining Chanto,
NIWAKA (USA), YEN (Paris).
378, Kameya-cho, Gokomachi-dori, Oike
agaru, Nakagyo-ku, Kyoto
Tel: 075-221-6403; fax: 075-221-6430
Email: vc3h-tjmr@asahi-net.or.jp
http://www.tsujimura-hisanobu.com/

Gen Yokoi
Born: 1957
Architectural Space Designer, a repre-
sentative of Souraku sha Inc.
Main projects include: Kuruma, Kushino
bo, Ginza An, Gyosai Sushi Dining,
Bar Hashimoto
#1001 Sunheim Minami Morimachi,
2-3-10, Tenjinbashi, Kita-ku, Osaka
Tel: 06-6356-4294; fax: 06-6356-4295
Email: so-inc@sun-inet.or.jp
http://www.sourakusha.com/